MW00656902

MY CONVERSION TESTIMONY

HOW ISLAM
LED ME BACK TO
CHRIST

CHARBEL RAISH

PAROUSIA
Proclaiming the fullness of Truth

Published and Distributed by Parousia Media PTY LTD
PO Box 59 Galston, NSW 2159
Ph: +61 2 9651 0375
office@parousiamedia.com
www.ParousiaMedia.com

ISBN 978-0-648198-43-7
ISBN 978-0-6481984-7-5 *eBook*

DEDICATION

To my mother Yvette Raish
Thanks for laying the foundations of faith in my life.
(And giving me that slap in the face!.. I needed it!)

CONTENTS

FOREWORD

Several years ago, an atheist - who had no intention of becoming Catholic - accompanied his fiancée, a fallen-away Catholic making her way back to the Church, to my RCIA class at the parish. Week after week, he would listen to the lectures intently but not engage in group discussions or ask any questions. Some months later, he approached me and asked if he could become a Catholic! I was quite surprised and a bit shocked since he had given no prior indication of being interested in the Catholic faith. When I asked how he came to this decision, he said that his discovery of the Catholic faith was like holding your hand in front of your face in a pitch-black room: "God was in front of me the whole time and I didn't see him. Your class helped me to see Jesus." I quickly interjected and explained that it was not my class but Christ's class. I told him that I was not teaching my opinion or theological speculation or hypotheses. I was simply teaching the one, holy, catholic and apostolic faith, the faith for which the early Church martyrs gave their lives. The key to his experience of Christ, I continued, was his being open to the Truth–the truth that the Holy Spirit had now emblazoned within his heart; the fullness of Truth that can only be found in the Catholic Church founded by Jesus Christ–the Way, the Truth, and the Life.

In our ongoing discovery of the nexus between faith and truth, we often have to take a few steps back before we can move forward. Parents of children who have fallen away from the Church often lament their child's decision, not understanding how such a thing could happen after years of investment in Catholic school education, driving their kids to and from youth group and Confirmation class every week, and taking them to Mass each Sunday. The reality is that many of these young adults do not know Jesus at all and are only fans of Christ, not true followers. Simply put: they are not in love with Jesus.

When we are in love, we cannot imagine our life without that person and seem to spend every waking moment thinking about being with the one we love. Many wayward Catholics, starving for true love and intimacy, drift into other religions or philosophical systems that they believe will fulfil the deepest longings and desires of their hearts. Like the disciples who walked away from Jesus after he said, "unless you eat the flesh of the Son of Man and drink his blood, you have no life within you" (John 6:53), who could "not endure sound teaching" (John 6:60), many young people "accumulate for themselves teachers to suit their own liking, and turn away from listening to the truth and wander into myths" (2 Timothy 4:3-4).

This is the story of Charbel Raish. God the Father is never at a loss for creativity in making His will known to us, and often uses the situations and circumstances of everyday life to bring us closer to Him. In Charbel's case, God used the practice of Islam. The pages that follow recount his personal journey of faith, his search for truth, and the discovery of his life's purpose—all profoundly relatable to the life experience of many Catholics today.

After a life-changing encounter with Christ, present Body, Blood, Soul, and Divinity in the Most Blessed Sacrament of the Eucharist, Charbel began to learn his faith and, more importantly, to *live* it with passion and conviction. He was responding to God's invitation to intimate, personal, loving, and life-giving communion—he was falling in love with Jesus! This newfound love-affair led Charbel to discern a call to the priesthood but, in God's providence, he met the woman God placed in his life to help him get to heaven and became a loving husband and dedicated father.

Now that Charbel's heart was completely open to God's will, he began to listen more deeply to the voice of the Lord and allowed the Holy Spirit to shape his life. In 2005, he started Parousia in his home and, like any new business venture, struggled to make it successful. At one point,

Charbel almost gave up hope. Through a lot of hard work and by God's grace, Parousia is now the most prominent Catholic evangelisation organisation in Australia, and one of the most influential in the world. Charbel's story is a personal testament to how God can use you if you are not afraid to abandon yourself completely to His will. I am honoured to have both a personal friendship with Charbel and professional relationship with Parousia since 2012, and my work in the Lord's vineyard has benefited greatly from our partnership.

My prayer is that Charbel's story will inspire those seeking answers to the deepest questions of their lives to turn toward Jesus so that they will know the truth that makes them free - free to become the person God created and calls them to be. I also pray that truth-seekers will come to understand that salvation comes from only one Source: the One True God - the God of Abraham, Isaac and Jacob; the God of Peter, James and John; the God of Muslims, Jews and Atheists - and He is none other than our Lord Jesus Christ! He is the God of Isaiah, who foretold His coming and who tells us that the Savior gave his back to those who beat him, his cheeks to those who plucked his beard, his face to buffets and spitting (cf. Isaiah 50:6). He is the God of Saint Paul who tells us that His name is above every other name, and that at the name of Jesus every knee should bend in heaven, on earth and under the earth, and that every tongue proclaim Jesus Christ is Lord to the glory of God the Father (cf. Philippians 2:10-11).

The truth and beauty of Sacred Scripture cry out to us loud and clear that the idols of men are merely silver and gold, the work of human hands. The psalmist describes the idols of this culture, e.g., cohabitation, contraception, euthanasia, so-called "alternative lifestyles" and pseudo-religions: "they have mouths but they cannot speak; they have eyes but they cannot see; they have ears but they cannot hear; they have nostrils but they cannot smell; with their hands, they cannot feel; with their feet, they cannot walk. No sound comes from their throats. Their makers will come to be like them and so will all who trust in them" (Psalm 115:5-8). Instead, let us follow the example of Christ, understanding that the greatest in God's eyes is the one who serves: the one who makes a gift of himself, who breaks himself open and pours himself out in love just as Jesus did on the Cross. With Charbel's incredible story as our backdrop and inspiration, let us take up our cross and follow Christ, for the cross is the meaning of sacrifice: the cross is the meaning of love.

Deacon Harold Burke-Sivers, M.T.S.,
Author, International Speaker,
Catholic Radio and
Television Personality

Endorsements

I first met Charbel at the West Coast biblical conference in L.A of January 2011. I was curious as to why this young man would travel so far for one conference. It turns out that he was visiting the states for much more than that and he was on a mission to network with lay-led apostolates as he himself was leading his own apostolate Parousia Media. We exchanged contact details and have been friends ever since. Charbel pointed out to me that he heard my conversion story so many years before along with the 3 cd set 'What is the Covenant?' which describes the relationship of the trinity with us as part of the family of God. One major difference Charbel discovered was that in Islam God is the all-powerful Master known as Allah and we are his slaves. In Christianity, we don't look at God as just master but as Father, Son and Holy Spirit. God is our father and we are His children. I encourage you to read this book and learn about a man who discovered in a real way to call upon God as Abba Father.

Dr Scott Hahn
Professor of Biblical Theology, Author, Founder of St Paul Centre

I have known Charbel since 2010 when he invited me to tour Australia to speak on the topic of Islam -- an important interest that we shared. Over the years we have maintained our friendship through his visits to the Eternal Word Television Network (EWTN), with many wonderful conversations. My own studies of the Qur'an, its background and the history of Islam helps me observe its similarities and important differences with the Bible and Christian doctrine. A more refined study of Islam is a necessary aid to serious dialogue with our Muslim brothers and sisters. Our personal friendship with Muslims is a crucial background for dialogue, but only when the non-Muslim understands the texts and terms of Islam makes possible a serious understanding of Islamic thought and ideology. I encourage you to get to learn more about Charbel and his search for the truth about God and humanity by reading his book. He learned more about cherishing and respecting Muslims as wonderful human beings made in the image and likeness of God, yet he learned this truth within the fullness of truth in the Catholic Church. He continues to share the good news of truth by evangelising across Australia and beyond through tools like Parousia and other means.

Fr Mitch Pacwa S.J.
EWTN Host, Author, Professor

Islam is a topic often avoided in conversation. It is politically charged and emotions can run high. Part of the reason is that people in the West are unfamiliar with Islam, having never read the Qur'an, entered a mosque or visited Muslim countries. The first time I met a Muslim was in Israel in 1995 but now my hometown in the USA has an ever-increasing population. It is incumbent on Christians to educate themselves and become conversant on the issue of Islam. My friend Charbel has had extensive contact with Muslims and understands them, their religion and their way of life. When I travelled throughout Australia with Charbel, his passion for the truth and love for the Catholic faith was palpable. His love for the Christian faith began when a Muslim friend challenged him about his beliefs. He didn't run away from the discussion but engaged his friend. As a result, it took him right to the point of reciting the shahada prayer but in that same day, he thankfully encountered Christ—and thus the title of this book. *How Islam Led Me Back to Christ* is a story of a young man that was searching for the truth and how God met him where he was. You will experience Charbel's struggles and how his trust in God led him to the fullness of faith in the Catholic Church. I recommend this book for knowledge of both Islam and Christianity.

Steve Ray
Speaker, Author, Pilgrimage Master

I have known Charbel for over ten years. Since my first visit to Australia in 2009 when he had me give sixteen talks in six days all over Sydney. There was a major highlight in that tour and it was at his parish of St Charbel's in Punchbowl. I gave a talk on Islam and we had over 1500 people attend, and this was a mid-week parish talk! There were Sunni and Shiite Muslims in attendance who I encouraged to ask me questions. And they did! It was a great night and an unforgettable tour. Charbel began to share his testimony with me during that tour and I was intrigued by the title he shared with me back then: "How Islam Led me back to Christ". He explained his choice of title by clarifying that it was his Muslim friends who challenged him concerning his faith. And it became a great blessing! He was compelled to do some serious soul searching and studying to defend his Catholic Faith. And that led him to experience Christ as never before. In this book, you will learn about the man, Charbel Raish, who has encountered God in a very real way. You will get a taste of the passion this man has for the Catholic Church that I have witnessed over many years of working with him during multiple trips down unda' and beyond! His passion has never waned. It is my prayer that his passion will rub off on all of us!

Tim Staples
Director of Apologetics for Catholic Answers

Charbel's conversion story is a passionate and deep one. It reminds me of why we should all treasure our Catholic Faith and never take it for granted. Conversion stories are always exciting and the Church more than ever needs to hear about them. Charbel's story also reminds me of why it is so important to restore apologetics as a core part of the Church's missionary work. The work of Parousia is a source of great joy for those in Australia and elsewhere who believe in apologetics. May Charbel and Parousia continue their great work for many more years to come.

Robert M. Haddad
Author of *Defend the Faith!*

Introduction

I thank God every day for my Muslim friends because if it were not for them I would probably have remained a lukewarm Catholic living a self-centred empty life focused on myself and indifferent to others. This would have ultimately led me to agnosticism, doubting whether or not there really is a God.

In this book, I will share the experience I had on that very day of visiting a mosque and how that visit led me to pray to God from my heart, for the first time in my life. I boldly asked for a sign, and guess what? I got it! Boy did I get it! It was all I needed to confirm that I was born into the true faith. I don't say that to disrespect those who follow other faiths, but I simply say it because it was the sign I needed to determine my purpose and to take my journey of faith to a whole new level which changed my worldview and perspective on life forever!

On that day in 1999, I began a journey in search for the fullness of Truth. I was led to prayer, study and action. I was yearning to share this treasure with all whom I encountered. I wanted to reach as many people as possible with this newly found truth! This experience led me to desire further study and to enter the seminary to discern if I had a vocation to the priesthood.

In this book, I will reflect on my days in school and on some of my post-school experiences. Six years after I left school I got engaged to my beautiful girlfriend Christine and we got married one year later. God has blessed me with such a beautiful and grace-filled wife. That same year I began an apostolate called Parousia Media. Christine and I now have 7 beautiful children and we practice and love the Catholic faith. Lots of things have happened in the last 14 years with Parousia Media that caused me to travel around the world to different countries where I have met so many wonderful people. They have come from all walks of life, with many moving stories of personal conversion that has led them to the great discovery that Jesus Christ is their Lord and Saviour.

To date, Parousia has reached over 350,000 people in person. I would never have dreamed that this was possible, but then, as the Gospel says; "...for with God nothing is impossible" (Luke 1:37). God is working unceasingly to draw us ever more firmly into His loving arms. If we only turn towards Him, God will do the rest.

My new journey of faith would not have happened

if not for the challenges I faced from my Muslim friends at Belmore Boys High School, Sydney. Therefore, it was appropriate that I title this book "How Islam Led Me Back to Christ". My prayer is that you will also be inspired, as I was, by reading a testimony that will showcase God's love and grace. May you also say "Yes" to His grace and get ready for what will be in store for you! God is moving faster than we can keep up with and so you'd better jump on the boat that is travelling with Him on the rapid river of grace. I pray that you will enjoy and be a part of this adventure of life! There has never been a dull moment in my life since accepting the truth. I have never been bored and never lost hope. I am truly happier and filled with joy, thanks be to the Lord Jesus Christ and all the graces He pours out into our souls through His Catholic Church. I hope that, at the very least, you will be encouraged to delve deeper into your faith as a result of reading this book! Enjoy.

CHAPTER 1

My Family Background and Upbringing

Born to Colombian and Lebanese Parents and the Foundational Years

He said to them, "Because of your little faith. For truly, I say to you, if you have faith as a grain of mustard seed, you will say to this mountain, 'Move from hence to yonder place,' and it will move, and nothing will be impossible to you."
(Matt 17: 20)

There is a very special reason why I was named Charbel, and that reason was based on a doctor's diagnosis when my mother was pregnant with me. About halfway through the pregnancy, mum began to bleed heavily for about a week. She was very worried and went to her doctor for a check-up. The doctor made it very clear that the bleeding was not good and that I had a less than 5% chance of survival to birth. He did not recommend that the pregnancy continue but mum was clear that she wanted to save her baby. The doctor said the only chance of the baby surviving would be if mum went home and remained to lie down almost all of the time. She was not to put her body under any stress whatsoever. Being an epileptic, mum would continue to have seizures which she also endured with her previous seven pregnancies. At this point in time, three children had already been miscarried and there was a very high chance that I would be her fourth miscarriage.

My mum immediately began praying to the "Doctor in Heaven" through the intercession of Saint Charbel, and she begged him with this prayer: "Saint Charbel, please help me to save this child. I don't want to lose another baby. I promise, if you ask God to save my child, I will name this baby in your honour. If it's a boy - Charbel; and if it's a girl - Charlene. I will also dress the baby in a black robe like yours for one year commencing on its first birthday. Please, Saint Charbel, intercede for me. I beg you. Amen".

The next day my mother stopped bleeding. I believe she was healed that night, through the intercession of Saint Charbel. She carried her pregnancy to full term and to the amazement of the doctor, I survived and was born completely healthy. Thanks be to God! Mum was not surprised. Extremely grateful, she wasted no time in taking me straight from the hospital to the church, even before going home. She held me at the front door of the church named in honour of the great saint - St Charbel's Monastery in Punchbowl, Sydney. My father called over one of the monks to give me a blessing. Then my mother carried me into the church and held me up in front of the altar thanking God for what He had done. She named me Charbel, as she had pledged. I was the first in my family to later be baptised and confirmed at this Maronite Catholic Church of St. Charbel.

As promised in her prayer, after one year mum dressed me in a small black robe like a monk and she has been grateful for my life ever since. Maybe not so much during my toddler years, for apparently I was a little terror and would not listen to mum! Oh well, mum never asked for "a good boy" just "a healthy" one! Thanks to her prayer asking for the intercession of Saint Charbel, I was born. She has no doubt about that and I am amazed at her strong faith. I am alive today thanks to that prayer. I have a purpose in life which is to tell people the story of God's work in each one of them. All this shows the importance of faith and the power of prayer. St Charbel, pray for us.

This is a famous image of St Charbel

Family Background

My father was born in March 1950, in Colombia, South America, where he lived with his Lebanese grandparents. He was the firstborn of 28 half brothers and sisters. That's right, my grandfather had lots of children with lots of women. He had 22 children with 7 Colombian women while my grandmother had 7 other children with her husband. So, my father has 28 siblings, and they are my uncles and aunties. Most of the family on both sides are currently living in either Cartagena or Barranquilla, Colombia. Abuela, my grandmother, is a native Colombian while my grandfather although born in Colombia, had Lebanese parents who settled there in the 1920s. When my father was 16 years old he was given the opportunity to travel with his grandfather and visit his grandparents' village Bnachii in Lebanon. That's where he met my mother.

My mother was born in 1953 in Kfarfo, North Lebanon. Mum had 13 siblings and grew up in poor circumstances. She was one of 14 children to the same parents and they would go to Church every Sunday and say their prayers at home. Her childhood longing was to be a nun; however, God had other plans. As was the tradition back then, the father of the boy would ask the father of the girl for her hand in marriage. Since my dad was travelling with his grandfather, he was the one to set things up. Within a year to the day of my father's arrival in Lebanon, my parents got married. Dad was 17 and mum was 14 and within six months they moved to Colombia. They had 2 boys in Colombia during the 6 years they were there, after which they migrated to Sydney, Australia, to meet mum's family. They settled in Belmore in Sydney during the '70s, where they had 4 more boys. So, I am the fifth of six boys in our family.

When I was a child my family would regularly visit

cousins and friends, go to Mass on Sundays, pray the rosary every night in English, Spanish and Arabic, as well as go to the Colombian and Lebanese picnic days which were always fun. My siblings and I would all be dressed the same way - navy blue suit or a sky blue suit. There was also a summer outfit that we all had to wear, combining cream shorts with the same white button-up shirt. People would comment on how nice we looked, dressed in the same outfits. Life did seem good and although mum was very strict we felt loved by both parents.

CHAPTER 2

Primary and High School

From a Catholic Primary School to a Public High School

Train up a child in the way he should go,
and when he is old he will not depart from it.
(Proverbs 22: 6)

I remember my mum and dad taking me to class on my first day of school at St Michael's Primary school in Belfield. Many of the students were crying as they didn't want their parents to leave, but I was very excited about finally going to school where my four older brothers had been going all my toddler life. I have a particular memory of looking back at mum and dad and smiling at them as they both smiled back at me. They seemed happy together back then.

I was known as 'Charlie' right from Kindergarten as my teacher had difficulty pronouncing 'Charbel' in my parent's

29

traditional way, which was to roll the tongue on the 'R'. Throughout my whole school life, I was known to everyone as Charlie. To this day, my family and friends still call me Charlie. I almost forgot my real name after a while.

I was just above average ability as a student. I was generally well behaved and got along with everyone, I certainly did not make enemies. St Michael's school had a compulsory weekly Mass on Fridays which was my only contact with the life of Church. I don't remember going to Sunday Mass during primary school.

In Grade 2, I received the Sacrament of Reconciliation at St Michaels whereby one confesses one's sins to a priest for the first time. We had classes leading up to this occasion, but sadly, that would be my last confession for almost eleven years. As a family, generally, we only went to Mass at St Charbel's during Christmas and Easter. I also recall that prayer in the home stopped for a period of time in my primary years. I know mum and dad were going through some tough times which might have been the reason that prayer wasn't enforced during that period.

In Grade 3, I made my first Holy Communion at St Michael's. I walked to the church by myself and then later my father and mother made it to the Mass - late, but they did make it. We have photos that were taken after Mass, for which I now treasure.

In Grade 6, we had our Confirmation classes. As the date drew closer for the celebration of Confirmation, I found out that I didn't need to participate - having been baptised in the Maronite Rite, the sacraments of Baptism and Confirmation are administered together. At the time, I didn't understand this; and remember feeling slightly left out during the school Confirmation Mass as I had to sit at the back of the group along with the non-Catholics who were not getting Confirmed. In my mind, it became clear to me that I was a Lebanese boy in an Australian school. I remember being the first boy in my grade to develop facial hair. I did feel slightly different but kept my friendships alive even after the year six graduation.

I should mention also that in Grade 5 a new Parish Priest by the name of Father Slattery was appointed to the parish of St Michael's in Belfield. With a mop of grey hair and beard, father Slattery looked stern but underneath the appearance was a holy priest with a big heart. He impressed upon the students and parishioners the need for reverence in Mass and the parish thrived under his direction. He introduced 24-hour Adoration of the Blessed Sacrament which involved at least one parishioner at a time spending an hour or more of personal prayer before Jesus in the Sacred Host. Someone always had to be there so there would never be an empty church even at two or three in the morning.

My brothers all followed rugby league and we were accustomed to playing tackle footy in the front yard all the time. In 1989 I was encouraged to play rugby league for my local club the Enfield Federals. I was eight years old and a very fast runner. I loved the training sessions. Although I had the speed, I was "skinny" and "soft" so I could not tackle properly or run the ball strongly. I was not only shy but also a little scared and not a good player at all. I was positioned on the wing and did not do much on the field that year. The following year I did not even make the team. I was so upset and quit rugby league for a few years. Three years later I thought I would give it another go and try out again, but I was dropped from the team as I was not a good player. This was discouraging at the time but I never gave up and later advanced in the sport during my high school years. So overall my primary school years were largely uneventful.

Belmore Boys High School

In 1994, I began attending the local public high school, where I remained until Year 12. We were sent there as we could not afford any other school and it was only a short walk from home. Apparently, the year before I entered this school, it was branded in news reports as 'the worst school in NSW' due to it having the poorest HSC results combined with a relatively high rate of crime and vandalism when compared to other schools. There were newspaper reports of students setting a teacher's hair on fire and of the Principal's office being set on fire as well. I remember there were fights every day and swearing was normal. I learnt new words that I never heard before. It was a school with 99% of the student body coming from a non-English speaking background. The school was one of the most culturally diverse places in Australia with students from all parts of the world. There were lots of refugee families that would label themselves "FOBs" which meant 'Fresh Off the Boat'. There were also problems with gangs and drug activity. I do want to clarify, however, that in listing these problems, it's easy to think that I must not have wanted to be there. I must say this is not how I felt. As I got to know the boys, I came to realise that each student had a good side to him and a capacity to develop good character if given the opportunity. I also discovered many of the teachers were fine people who were genuinely concerned that I develop to the best of my ability. I never felt unsafe at Belmore Boys.' I began to feel more comfortable among my peers. I knew that I would be respected by them provided I treated them similarly.

I learned that some teachers feared for their life knowing that if they were to put a boy on detention the "payback" would be a smashed-up car in the car park. So teachers who were not in control had to be careful how to discipline. Some of the senior students were much older, almost the same age as the new teachers, because they had to repeat their grades several times before moving up to the next grade. So, it wasn't uncommon to hear stories of 'personal relationships' between those older students and a few of their teachers. I remember also hearing about a death in the class, at least once a year. If it wasn't a car accident it was a shooting or stabbing or serious sickness. One class member of mine is doing time in jail for his involvement in gang-raping a teenage girl. He is serving Australia's longest sentence for such a crime. Another student from our school was Andrew Chan, who was killed by firing squad in Bali a few years ago. He was one of the leaders of the "Bali 9" who was accused of smuggling drugs into Bali. The story made news headlines for many years as he spent ten years in jail before finally being executed. Apparently, he had a spiritual conversion to Christ during his time in jail - this is really special, and I pray that he now shares in God's glory in heaven, as indeed I pray that we will all enjoy the face-to-face vision of God in heaven for all eternity.

My best friends were either Muslim or Orthodox Christian, but I don't recall having any Catholic friends. I mentioned that in my primary school years I felt different being a Lebanese person in a predominantly Australian school. Although in high school I was among many Lebanese students, I still felt like I didn't fit in, as they were all Muslim Lebanese. I had no Catholic Lebanese friends.

Many people thought I was Islamic just because I was Lebanese. One Muslim student, Rami, in particular, had a very positive impact on me and I remember respecting him for his example of faithfulness. This was demonstrated during a P.E lesson on "safe sex" and how to use condoms when Rami refused to participate because of his religious beliefs on the topic. Knowing him to be a practising Muslim and one of the most prayerful people in the school, I admired his conviction in his faith and his courage in making this bold decision.

Although I felt like an outsider coming from a Catholic primary school, I found a way through sport to connect with the boys after the first term. I built up the courage to play rugby league again and since my body was growing and I was trying to impress to "fit in". I had to step up and not be scared to tackle. I did end up playing rugby league which really became a big part of my life and my identity. I not only played for my local club the Enfield Federals (yes I finally made the side!), but I also played for Belmore Boys'. My sport gave me a new acceptance and popularity as I had speed and my confidence was growing. I played upper grade and for the rep teams at school. I was scoring tries and setting them up. I would later become the Captain of our school team and by the time I was 16 I was not just on the wing but I had played every position on the field and was a real leader in the team. One of my teammates was a devout Muslim who was always asking me questions about Christianity - not to get answers but to show me its flaws. This became a common part of my conversations with my Muslim friends throughout high school.

One of the first questions I got from my Muslim friends was "what is that around your neck"? I was wearing a gold crucifix on a chain and I would respond "it's Jesus". They would say "Yes I know but why is he on the cross? Don't you know he didn't really die on the cross?" I would respond by saying "that's news to me as I thought he did." My Muslim friends responded by saying "Jesus was on the cross but he didn't die as Judas replaced him on the cross and people thought it still was Jesus because of all the blood." It was interesting for me to hear that Judas the betrayer was the one to replace Jesus on the cross. It was also interesting to hear that according to Islam, Jesus didn't die but was assumed into Heaven. I also heard that Jesus was coming back to earth one day, but not as Judge (for only Allah can judge) but to reveal to the world that He didn't die on the cross and that Islam is the true religion. One other thing I was told is that Jesus is going to get married as he didn't get married the first time he was on earth. I should point out at this point I was not really convinced about these assertions but found them to be interesting, nonetheless. Another Islamic theory is that Jesus was on the cross but did not die, he was only unconscious and that's why he was seen alive and walking around three days later. I found this idea very interesting too. The reason why I could not see through all these denials of the truth about Christ was that I had an inadequate catechesis regarding the Easter events myself.

So many questions which were posed to me, such as, "Who is Jesus to you?" and "How can God be human?", or "How can God have a son?" etc. I will go through these questions in more detail in the next chapter, as the sheik, I met later asked the exact same questions. So as you can see there was a lot happening during my high school years. I had so many life-lessons at Belmore Boys'.

My first job through high school was at McDonald's in customer service. I joined a taekwondo school at Malik Fahad school with my friends and I was kept busy in Rugby League training for both club and school. Having to work a few days a week, with martial arts training as well, my time was very much occupied with activities. In all of this, I was blessed to get along with people I met no matter what their background.

In October 1999, I sat the Higher School Certificate (HSC) Examinations. I was keen to do well, so as to leave highschool having achieved something. My friends were not motivated to get high marks and had no intention of going to university. I remember some boys would put their name on the exam paper and then sleep through the sessions. After our first exam day which was English, we all celebrated as we had the first one out of the way. We didn't care to get good grades, we were just happy to finish the exam. We still had the rest of the HSC to do. I did not do well in the exams, passing only 3 subjects. I failed half the subjects and was ranked in the bottom 30% of the state. Being the school captain it was not a good look to have had such a bad score. Throughout high school, I was always an above-average student and came first in some subjects each year. I had myself to blame for not studying properly or asking the right questions. I did not have the discipline to sit in class and focus for too long. My mind would wander off or we would not listen to the teacher and muck around. The school was fun because of the friendships and laughs we had. I have kept in touch with my friends since high school and as much as I may have wasted my time or pointed out how bad the school's reputation was, I can say I learnt so many life lessons that would stay with me until today. Thank you Belmore Boys High!

CHAPTER 3

The Day at the Mosque

Christ's Voice in the Church that Day

*But you are a chosen race, a royal priesthood, a
holy nation, God's own people, that you may declare
the wonderful deeds of him who called you out of
darkness into his marvellous light. (1 Peter 2:9)*

During the first semester in Year 12, a guest speaker came
to the school. His name was Sheik Ahmed. I was invited to
attend a talk he was giving to the Muslim students. It was
an easy way to get out of class so I decided to go. I thought
I had nothing to lose. Every Muslim student seemed to be
there which was over half the school. This guest speaker
spoke with authority and passion. He had the attention of
the whole group. I remember looking around the hall and
couldn't believe that these students - many of whom I knew
had committed crimes - would all sit in silence respecting
this religious man while the rest of the time they would

be horribly disrespectful to the teachers in class. Sheik Ahmed was respected by all the boys and that impressed me. The only point I remember him saying was how the Qur'an was prophetic. It had remarkable details of things like the solar system and the fact that bees have more than one stomach. Once the session was finished I was invited to visit Sheik Ahmed at the Mosque. I agreed to go and so my friend Ali took me to see him.

Ali took me to a room upstairs at the back of the Mosque where some men were sitting on the floor eating lunch. There were sheets of butcher paper spread across the floor with over a dozen men eating and sharing the food. They invited me to join them so I sat down to eat. The serving for lunch was salad and meat. I put some salad on my plate but they noticed I didn't take any meat. They questioned me about this, and I told them that I was fasting from meat, but they couldn't understand how I was fasting when I was still eating salad. They explained to me that during Ramadan, Muslims fast from sunrise to sunset from all food and drink for a whole month. "Which way is real fasting, the Muslim or Christian way, they asked me?" I could not argue with them at the time so I agreed with them, that the Muslim way was better. It was at this point that I noted in the back of my mind that it was 1 - 0 on the scoreboard to the Muslims.

I was a competitive person and loved my scoreboards

so I turned this meeting into a challenge thinking that I could actually convert this Muslim leader to the Christian faith, without even knowing it very well myself. I was wrong, and as you will see, the opposite happened. You might also be wondering why I was fasting when I was not otherwise taking my faith very seriously at that point. It was actually through witnessing for six years my Muslim friends faithfully practice Ramadan that really inspired me. How these guys, who would often be caught on the wrong side of the law, would increase their prayer and fasting during the month of Ramadan was remarkable. Ramadan is not just about fasting but also about trying to be more spiritual and committed to the demands of the Islamic faith. The fact that crime rates in the area dropped during that month of Ramadan also impressed me. In my final year, I asked my mum how we fast as Christians and she told me about the tradition of abstaining from meat on Fridays, which I did in my final year of school during Lent. From that year on, Lent became a time of renewal for me. During each Lenten season, I felt a strong impulse to try to deepen my commitment to all that my Catholic faith called me to.

Once lunch was finished, they cleaned up the food, put away the butcher's paper and we sat on the floor in the corner of the room with Sheik Ahmed and my friend Ali. The sheik asked me "how do you pray?" I began to recite the "Our Father" but when I got halfway through it he stopped me and said "don't insult God. He is not a father." He then asked me whether I had a dad, and said, "If you have an earthly father why would you put human attributes on God?" I simply said, I don't know and again, in the back of my mind, I noted another point to the Muslim side. It was now 2 - 0. The Sheik then asked me who taught me the "Our Father". I said, "Jesus taught it to me." The sheik then said, "Who is Jesus to you?" I replied, "God". He then asked whether Jesus was God or just the Son of God. I said, "both I think". "Why would God be human and how is that possible?" he replied. I had no idea how to answer him as I felt it sounded weird that God could become a man. He pushed further asking, "did God leave heaven to come on earth? And while on earth who was looking after the world?" Again I had nothing and he was racking up the points. It was now over 5-0 on my personal scoreboard.

The questions continued "was Jesus talking to himself when he taught you that prayer? If Jesus is God and he is praying that means God is praying to Himself?" That also sounded strange to me. He then went on to say "you Christians also believe in the Trinity, don't you?" I said "yes we do. The Father, Son and Holy Spirit." But he said, "so you believe in three gods?" I said "No it's one God" but the Sheik came back and said, "you see how confused you are, it's clearly three gods and there can only be one God". I could not reply to him. I had never learnt how to explain the mystery of the Holy Trinity in a convincing way. The sheik continued with his questions. "If Jesus died on the cross, then that meant he could not be God because God can't die." I replied by saying, "Jesus rose from the dead," but he responded by saying "even if that's the case, there is no proof for the resurrection because how can God die to begin with? We would all cease to exist instantly." "How can God have a son? Where there is a father there must be a mother and it makes no sense for God to have a son. It's impossible."

There were many more questions which themselves could fill a whole book but one of them was this: "Who looks more like Jesus, Muslims or Christians?" After all, Jesus had a gown and beard and most of the Muslims had a beard, and the religious ones had a gown. I agreed with him Muslims look more like Jesus and then he said: "Who looks more like Mary, Muslims or Christians?" You see Mary had a veil and Muslim women wear a hijab which looks the same. I thought at the time that it wasn't a great argument because it's what's on the inside that counts, but the Sheik said that was just another reason to show how true Islam is. As you can see I had no idea how to respond and because of this, the Sheik felt I was ready to convert.

Now that the sheik could see that I was not coming back with any questions, he asked me to do one more thing. He said, "I want you to close your eyes and say three times in Arabic there is only one God and His prophet Muhammad." So I did "La illah ou il Allah ou Muhamed resul Allah." I opened my eyes and he said: "Ah I can see your eyes are different, you have a light coming from you." I said I don't feel any different but he then gave me a towel and a white gown. "I want you to have a shower and wash your old life away and start anew. Welcome brother" he said. I didn't know what to say so I went to the shower and began to wash. I was nervous as I was now officially a Muslim. According to Islam, the prayer I said was the Shahada which is one of the Five Pillars of Islam and the 'baptism', if you like, to be initiated into the religion. I thought to myself that since I could not explain Islam and everything the Sheik said made sense along with six years of Islamic influence, then I must be destined to become a Muslim. As I was having the shower I wanted to pray and so the only prayers I could say were the Our Father and Hail Mary. I started to pray ten Hail Mary's, which is a decade of the Rosary. By the time I began to put the gown over my head I was finishing my last Hail Mary with 'Amen'. It was at this moment I heard a whisper: "Not Yet. Not Yet." I still wonder to this day if it was the voice of Our Lady whom I had invoked through prayer. I took off the gown and put my normal clothes back on.

I came out of the bathroom and the sheik asked, "what's wrong? Why won't you wear the gown? We are about to pray, come join us." I told him that I did not know my faith and it would not be fair for me to leave a religion without knowing why. I need to study it first, and if God wants me to be a Muslim then I will answer that call because I want the truth. Then I asked him to please pray for me. "Of course we will, no problem," the Sheik said. I felt an urge to put one question to him. "Can I ask you a question please?" He said, "yes you can ask me anything." I asked, "how can God allow a man to marry 4 wives?". He said "ah that's a good question. Not any man can marry 4 wives, but only those who treat them each equally." I asked, "how can you love them equally?" He said, "Do you have other brothers or sisters?" I said "yes". He then said, "does your mother love you all equally?" I said, "yes, but that's a different type of love." I could see that love between spouses is very different from the love between parents and children. He said, "Love is Love". I felt that was not a satisfactory answer and put a point on the Christian side, so it was like 10-1. I thanked the sheik for his time and went home.

It was late when I got home from school after my discussion with the Sheik and mum asked me where I was. I said "just down at the local mosque," and she slapped me across the face, shouting "What!". I said "Yes! I wanted to speak to the Sheik as I have so many questions. I am very confused. I think God is calling me to be a Muslim mum." She said, "go to the church now and ask Jesus if He wants you to be a Muslim because He is also in the Qur'an so He will have the answer for you. If He says to be a Muslim then I won't stop you." I said to myself, "that's fair enough," so I began my walk to the church which was only ten minutes away. I was so torn and not sure what God wanted of me. I had this heavy weight on my shoulders and could not even breathe properly. The 10-minute walk felt like an hour. When I finally arrived at St Michael the Archangel Catholic Church in Belfield, the doors were unlocked. It is very rare to find churches open in the evenings. Thankfully this church was open and I walked inside not knowing that my life was going to change forever.

When I went into the church I could see the crucifix erected high at the front and directly under it was the golden box which I now know is called a 'Tabernacle'. Next to the 'Tabernacle' was a red light flickering and I remember when I was in primary school, a teacher said that whenever you see the red light, it means that Jesus is there. Well, the candlelight was on and I wondered if He must be there. I knelt down at the back of the church and looked straight at the 'Tabernacle'. I said the following words, "Jesus, if you are really here, show me. Do you want me to be a Christian or a Muslim?" I was looking for a sign and all I could do was stare fixated at the 'box' on the altar. I could not get my eyes off that 'box' and was waiting expectantly for a sign. I didn't hear or feel anything for about thirty minutes. After thirty minutes an elderly lady came in, to light a votive candle and I thought to myself "Wow! What a holy woman... she is going to heaven". Almost instantly I had a flashback to a discussion with my Muslim friends about salvation. According to Islam, when you die you will meet your judge immediately and the only way to enter heaven is to answer these 3 questions which the judge will ask of you:

1) Who is the real God? The answer being Allah. The word Allah is necessary as that is the given name in the Qur'an and you can't say God or Elohim or Yahweh etc, it is simply Allah.

2) Who is his prophet? Of course, you must answer Muhamed.

3) What is the true religion? The answer needs to be Islam.

I was told that if you get any one of those questions wrong you will go down to the hellfire so you must get all three right. I thought to myself "This lady is not going to answer those questions correctly, according to Islam. That means she is going to Hell!" I felt that couldn't be right. So, I looked back at the 'tabernacle,' never thinking of what was going to happen next.

As I was looking at the tabernacle a black and white shadow of a face began to appear. It became clear that it had a beard and looked like Jesus. I looked away and then back again but the image would not go away. I then heard an internal voice say "Charbel, are you going to give up all that I have done for you?" I knew that the voice had to be Jesus and He was asking me if I was willing to turn my back on all the blessings I had received from my Catholic upbringing, to join Islam? Was I going to turn my back on all those miracles worked by Jesus that are recounted in the Bible and that my mother had also told me so much about? I had to answer the voice and decide there and then. I said to Jesus, "No Lord. I am not going to give you up". At that moment, the weight was lifted from my shoulders and I could breathe properly again. I said to myself, "I am a Catholic and I will remain a Catholic but now I need to know why".

Having now received the sign I had asked for, I made my decision to remain Catholic. I still did not understand much about the Catholic Faith but I got a strong enough sign to stay and explore it further. That image on the 'Tabernacle' disappeared. I later discovered that it was the mysterious image on the Shroud of Turin. I could not ask for a more perfect image to appear before me at that time in my life. I have been told by some that I was just 'seeing things' and it could have just been a reflection from the way the light reflected on the 'Tabernacle'. That's a possibility, but even if it was, God still used it to imprint an image of Christ in my mind. Even after looking away and looking back at the 'Tabernacle' the image was still there for a few minutes. I can still picture the image today and I am so blessed to have seen this Shroud of Turin image. Once I had found out what the sign meant, I was more determined than ever to learn more about my faith.

It happened that out of all the churches in Australia, this particular church had a faith formation night with guest speakers every Friday. It was called 'Lumen Verum Apologetics': a group of adults who would meet every Friday night to listen to a guest speaker defending a different aspect of the Catholic Faith. This program had been running in the parish for three years. I started to recall some memories of those same people whom I had seen in the church when I was dragged to the 'Holy Hours' with mum who began to go back to church years later and my younger brother Joey. I remember noticing a tall man come into the church, walk up to the sanctuary, and walk into the sacristy (where the priest gets ready for Mass) and come out with a small box, then walk out of the church and go around to a classroom in the primary school. I also noticed back then, a group of adults meeting in that area, as I could see through the open windows from the right side of the church. There was also at times a shorter stocky man doing the same thing as this taller man. After going for the first time in my life to listen to a talk on the faith, I recognised those same two men. The first tall guy was Robert Haddad, a school teacher and also a good friend of mine. The second person was David Obeid who also was a school teacher and is still now a good friend of mine. These two men were exactly the people I needed to meet at that time. These are arguably our country's best Catholic Apologists when it comes to explaining the faith, especially to our protestant brothers and sisters. They can quote bible verses and clearly describe Church teaching. The founder of this group, Arlette Bowen, a mother and former Olympic athlete from the inner west Sydney was another inspiration and she would organise the guest speakers, flyers, bulletin announcements, set up the hall, posters, introduce the speaker, open and close in prayer and put a collection box out. She is still to this day organising talks there on a monthly basis. I learned so much from Lumen Verum and made a commitment to go every Friday. I also remember how impressed I was to see other young Maronite Catholics, close to my age, attending these same talks. Finally, I could meet Lebanese Catholics who looked like me and loved their faith.

I want to acknowledge the men who inspired me during this period in my life, when I made that initial return to the Church, in addition to the three people I already mentioned in the previous paragraph. I am grateful for having met these young men of faith who would consistently attend these talks in those early years. Just seeing them there was encouraging for me. These talks gave me an opportunity to ask lots of questions and build up a sense of belonging through the fellowship of these committed Catholics. I finally found my home. I found my parish. I found my group of friends to encourage me. I found the answers to my questions. I would ask questions like "how do we know Jesus died on the Cross?" "How can God become a man?" "How can we explain the Holy Trinity?" "Isn't that 3 gods?" "How can three also be one?" "Why do we call God 'Father?'" "Can God have a son?" I wanted answers to all of those questions that were presented to me during high school, which I could not then answer. Now that I heard all of the answers, I kept coming back for more. I loved every moment of it. Lumen Verum would become my regular source of nourishment and St Michael's at Belfield would be my home away from home for my prayer life and regular Mass and confession beyond my school years.

CHAPTER 4

Post High School

My Longing to Spread the Faith

*O God, thou art my God, I seek thee, my soul thirsts
for thee; my flesh faints for thee, as in a dry and
weary land where no water is. (Psalm 63:1)*

When I left school I made a commitment to attend Lumen
Verum Apologetics each Friday. I would find myself sitting
in these lectures for ninety minutes or more, plus question-
and-answer sessions. How was it that I could not sit for
forty-five minutes at school, but on these Friday night
lectures I would sit for more than double the time? It was
because I wanted the answers. I accepted the fact that I did
not know my faith and I wanted to try and do something
about this. I wanted to respond to my Muslim friends who
had questioned me about Jesus Christ, God and the Holy
Trinity. I committed to going to Mass on Sundays and
I went to Confession for the first time since making my

First Confession as an eight-year-old. At that time Father Slattery was the parish priest and he was a good influence on me. During the year 2000, I worked full-time in a sports administration traineeship for Classic Sportswear. During Lent in the year 2000, I made a further commitment to visit the church every day. My mum would go to a prayer group each night from 11pm to midnight praying the Rosary, Divine Mercy Chaplet, and some other prayers along with the Stations of the Cross for Lent. I committed to going every night during Lent and I made it on most of those nights.

Also, during that year of 2000, I attended a course on philosophy and theology at the Centre for Thomistic Studies in Sydney. I was so fulfilled in learning more about my faith and could not get enough of it. I kept going to talks whenever they were being presented and I felt a growing desire to spread the faith. Prior to this, I had not yet been completely committed to the faith. The year 2000 was, therefore, a turning point for me; all my doubts began to evaporate as I became more and more convinced that all of the Church's teaching was true. It was all finally making sense in my head. I still had to undergo the next stage, which was the conversion of my heart. God was still working on me.

During Lent 2000 to 2001 I went to Mass every day and also the Holy Hour at night. I was invited by a friend,

Paul, to go to the Youth Mass at St Charbel's Church and get to know other young Maronite Catholics. We planned to distribute Rosary beads and holy cards. I was not as confident as my friend, but I can say that after Paul came into my life I came out of my shell and was much more confident in professing my faith. Paul was organising the praying of the Rosary in people's homes, and we did a "thirty-three-day consecration to Jesus through Mary," as laid down by St Louis De Montfort. We had a retired priest meet with us at the church, who led us in prayer. That retired priest would later become one of my best friends. His name was Father Chris and he was a former Benedictine monk.

In Lent 2001, I was consecrated to Mary and enrolled in the Brown Scapular thanks to Father Chris and my friend Paul. Paul was so in love with God and Our Lady and he wanted to do as much as he could. I was encouraged by that. Seeing another young person so engaged in his prayer life and loving it as I did, was such a boost for me. I was joining Paul in going to the Chapel at the house of Father Chris where we prayed the Divine Office and attended Mass. I was introduced to the Liturgy of the Hours and the ordinary Novus Ordo Mass in both English and Latin facing East. I had time to immerse myself in prayer for hours each day. I laughed with my mum because only a year earlier I was saying I did not enjoy prayer and now I couldn't get enough of it! This had to be God's grace; there was no other explanation.

So now, just over a year and a half out of high school and I found myself in church twice a day, not including the chapel at the house of Father Chris. Prayer life included daily Mass, Divine Office twice a day, a Holy Hour, three Rosaries, the Chaplet of Divine Mercy, going to talks, prayer groups at people's homes and doing Bible studies with Father Chris. In addition to this, I enrolled in a Religious Education Certificate course at the Catholic Adult Education Centre in Lidcombe and continued attending the courses at CTS. I was also introduced to Scott Hahn thanks to a cassette tape given to me by Father Chris. The set was called 'Evangelising the Baptised: Calling Catholics to Become Bible Christians and Vice Versa'. A three-cassette set, and it ignited my love for listening to talks in the car. I wanted more and went back to Father Chris for more titles. I even remember the second set, it was called 'What is the Covenant?' This was one of my favourites as it explained the family based on marriage as an image of the Trinity. I would visit Father Chris to listen to these cassettes as well and begin Bible studies with Paul and Father Chris at his house. We studied Genesis, Exodus, Matthew, Mark, Luke and John as well as the Book of Revelation. I can't tell you how hungry I was to learn more and pray more and evangelise all those I met and enjoy the fellowship with believers. I could say that I was on a spiritual high, on fire for God and His Church.

With all of this spiritual nourishment, a group of us wanted to share our faith and experiences with others. Paul had the idea of starting another apologetics group, aimed at young adults, at St Charbel's in Punchbowl. He got approval from the Superior and came up with the name for the group, "*Guardians*". I remember that day clearly - it was June 13, 2001. Both Paul and I were setting up for the very first 'Guardians' talk which featured Father Terence Naughtin on the topic "The Four Last Things." The first night was focussed on "death and judgement" while the next fortnight would concentrate on "Heaven and Hell". We set up thirty chairs, not sure of how many people would attend the first talk. Exactly forty people came that night; we were so happy with that turnout. We had to put out a few more chairs. I would ring around my friends to invite them to the talks. I had something to bring my mates to, as well as introducing them to an enjoyable night that was very informative and stimulating. Guardians would go on for another eighteen years, with guest speakers each fortnight. This was another big part of my personal formation.

Once Guardians began I would plan with Father Chris a document on how to promote the nights. Father Chris would attend the nights to hear confessions and he was always kept very busy with that part of the event. The nights would grow from forty each fortnight to an average of eighty people. There were some hot topics covered at times. In those early years, the two most popular talks were 'Jesus or Muhammad' presented by Raymond De Souza, with almost three hundred in attendance, and another talk on 'Answering Islam' presented by Robert Haddad which had over three hundred people in the audience. Following from these beginnings, I would then start a ministry called Parousia Media, bringing international speakers to present talks at Guardians. Those nights would attract audiences of 800 or even 1,500, with speakers such as Tim Staples. I'll describe the work of Parousia later in the book. At the time, however, both Charbel Labban a good friend of mine that I met at Father Chris's place and I would work on a pamphlet with Father Chris and offered to design posters and flyers to hand out at Mass on Sundays.

My church life and my social life were united. I encountered new people and groups every day. I discovered my Maronite Church and it was alive! With the monks at St Charbel's combining morning prayer and evening prayers with Mass every day we had two options for Mass. There would be Confession available during each Mass and Guardians every second Wednesday. The Rosary was prayed every evening, and this was also the case at St Joseph's Maronite Church and St Michael's in Belfield. With the two Maronite churches nearby plus St Michael's and Father Chris, I was completely plugged into the life of the Church in both Rites.

At this stage, I began to be asked by people who saw my involvement in the Church, whether I wanted to be a priest. With all the hours I was spending in prayer each day, as well as focusing my social life among active believers, my family could see what was going on. I personally, however, wanted to get married. Whenever I would talk to young ladies at church, I was always thinking in the back of my mind, and wondering if one of them would make a good wife. There were certainly a good number of devout women who were like me in age and I was open to dating and pursuing a relationship, but I was so busy with work, prayers and evangelising - that was the priority for me.

One day Paul asked me a direct question about my vocation: "Do you want to be a priest?" I said, "No, I want to get married." He said that he was going to join the priesthood. I was impressed to see him want to make that commitment. He invited me to a discernment retreat in the middle of 2002. This was for men who were discerning whether or not they might have a vocation to the priesthood. I reluctantly went to it knowing I was called to marriage, but with so many people mentioning the priesthood to me, maybe it was a sign from God.

I continued to think about a vocation to the priesthood and the question my mother put to me was, "Into which Rite will you be studying for the priesthood?" That really was a tricky question because I spent my time growing up at St

Michael's at Belfield in the Roman Rite and apart from the Christmas and Easter Masses, and Mass as a toddler, I had recently discovered the Maronite Church in a significant way. Most people thought the Maronite Rite would be the obvious choice. While I was discerning whether to enter the seminary, I remember meeting a beautiful girl who had such a contagious smile, at one of the Guardians evenings. I was introduced to her by Ingrid Azzi, who was someone I met at the CTS classes and had seen around the church. Ingrid hadn't been so friendly to me before this particular night, and I remember her being extra friendly this time as she introduced me to her friend Christine Haddad. I had not seen this girl at Guardians before and gladly welcomed her to the group, internally thinking "Wow!" She had long dark hair and was in a business outfit. I remember thinking to myself how attractive Christine was but how she was also a sister in Christ. If I was called to the priesthood, I thought I had to look at all women as sisters if I was not going to be able to get married. I had to give God a chance to show me whether I was called to the celibate life or not. I got Christine's email and added it to the Guardians database. I would go on to see Christine at different church functions and prayer groups. I was always attracted to her but knew I was not going to pursue anything while discerning a possible vocation to the priesthood.

CHAPTER 5

My Debate with My Muslim Friend

Bible and Qur'an Discussion in the Shopping Centre

*Always be prepared to make a defence to anyone
who calls you to account for the hope that is in you,
yet do it with gentleness and reverence.*
(1 Peter 3:15)

About a year-and-a-half after leaving school, I received a phone call from my Muslim friend. He said he was reading the Bible and that we Christians should be reading the Bible correctly, as Jesus does not claim to be God there. I was happy to meet up with him and discuss this further, as I had just spent two years attending Lumen Verum Apologetics and listening to Scott Hahn cassettes as well as completing some basic introductory courses on theology and philosophy. So we set up a meeting that week and he presented his Qur'an and I presented my Bible. We were sitting in a shopping centre nearby and opened up the start of each book. He opened up his Qur'an and it read...

1. *In the name of Allah, the Beneficent, the Merciful*
2. *Praise be to Allah, Lord of the Worlds*
3. *The Beneficent, the Merciful*

Then I opened up the Bible and it read...

1. *In the beginning, God created the heavens and the earth.*
2. *The earth was without form and void, and darkness was upon the face of the deep; and the Spirit of God was moving over the face of the waters.*
3. *And God said, "Let there be light"; and there was light.*

I mentioned some of the differences between them, how the Bible starts with the story of creation and then expands from there. The Qur'an, however, begins by invoking God but is written in a way that is clearly from a narrator (Muhammad) giving instructions. There is no chronological order and there are no real details about the stories taken from the Torah and New Testament (Injeel in Arabic). The Qur'an simply refers to them rather than describing what happened in detail. It contains many statements within the same 'sura' (chapter) where it states one thing and in the next verse, it continues onto something else, completely unrelated. I told my friend it is hard to read the Qur'an and he said there are interpreters that can help you, that is, they provide the lens through which to read it. I suggested to my friend that we go back to the time before these books were even written and ask this question...

NOTE! *Before I write this particular question, I will highlight the other questions I asked in the ensuing conversation, by putting in bold text who is speaking. This is so you can find them easily in the future. I will put the word* **ME** *when I speak, and the words* **MUSLIM FRIEND** *when he speaks. This is how we continued the conversation...*

Trinity and Origins of God

ME : What was God doing before He created the world?
I continued, "Think about it, because God always existed for all eternity. At some point, He decided to create. Before He created the world we could not call Him the creator. Before He created the world He had nobody else to be the all-powerful master over. Before He created the world there was no one to be Lord over, which prompts the question as to what He was then doing and who He is in

His essence?"

MUSLIM FRIEND: We can't ask that question because it's not in the Qur'an.

ME: Can you admit that God loves us?

MUSLIM FRIEND: Yes, He does.

ME: What is love?

MUSLIM FRIEND: Being nice to people. Doing good things.

ME: Does God need us?

MUSLIM FRIEND: Yes He does, we are His slaves and He is our master.

ME: Did God need us from all eternity? He was perfectly happy before creating us.

MUSLIM FRIEND: We are not allowed to ask that question.

ME: God does not need slaves to do work for Him. For all eternity He was perfectly happy and self-sufficient. There is no point to us being here only by accident. At some point in history Allah decided to create, but for what purpose?

MUSLIM FRIEND: Allah is our master and we are His slaves on earth. We serve Him and nobody else. We are not an accident as Allah willed our existence so we can serve Him.

ME: Whatever was existing from all eternity created us not because it needs slaves but for one reason only, love. This being is Allah who didn't start loving at the time of creation but always loved from all eternity.

MUSLIM FRIEND: Yes, God loves us and yes, whatever He does now He was always doing as He does not change.

ME: If God always loved then who was He loving before He created us?

MUSLIM FRIEND: Nobody else just Himself.

ME: That is not love if you are loving yourself. Love is when you give of yourself to another person.

MUSLIM FRIEND: There was no other person before creation.

ME: If you are true 'love' then you have to love another person. Person 1, loved Person 2, and Person 2 received that love and returning that love back to Person 1 becoming a 3rd person. The love between the two is so perfect and infinite that the love itself is a person.

MUSLIM FRIEND: I still don't understand

ME: We call the first Person God the Father, who gives of Himself totally to the Second Person, God the Son. God the Son returns that love totally in God the Holy Spirit. There can only be three persons in Allah not 1, 2 or 4. It must be three if He is love.

MUSLIM FRIEND: We are forbidden to ask these questions outside of the Qur'an. I will lose my religion if we did ask those questions.

ME: We know God loves us because He does not need us. From all eternity God loved as a family of Father, Son and Spirit. Mysteriously, at some point in eternity, He consummated that love and begot children through His creation and that's us.

MUSLIM FRIEND: Yes, we are slaves of Allah but also children in a way because we are His creation. But God Himself does not have a son.

How Can Jesus be the Son of God?

ME: I remember in school you used to tease me that God can't have a son. But in the Qur'an Mary is a virgin, so who is the father of Jesus?

MUSLIM FRIEND: He has no father.

ME: Where there is a mother there has to be a father. Who made Mary pregnant?

MUSLIM FRIEND: God made Mary pregnant

ME: So who is the father of Jesus?

MUSLIM FRIEND: Nobody.

ME: If God made Mary pregnant, who is the father of Jesus?

MUSLIM FRIEND: I told you Jesus has no father. Mary got pregnant from the spirit of Allah.

ME: Bingo! You agree with us Christians that the spirit of God came down and made Mary pregnant. That's the Holy Spirit.

MUSLIM FRIEND: I said the spirit of God, not the Holy Spirit

ME: We call the spirit of God the Holy Spirit. *Ruah, Allah. Ruah el Kudus.*

MUSLIM FRIEND: I know what you are saying but that does not mean the spirit of God is separate to Him. There are not two gods just one.

ME: The Spirit of God is, in fact, God, just as much as the Father is God and the Eternal Son is God. It was through the power of the Holy Spirit, sent by the Father, that the Eternal Son was conceived in the womb of the Blessed Virgin Mary, thereby uniting to Himself a human nature: "The Holy Spirit will come upon you, and the power of the Most High will overshadow you; therefore the child to be born will be called holy, the Son of God." (Luke 1:34-35).

The *Catechism of the Catholic Church* describes

beautifully the incarnation of the Son of God in the womb of the Virgin Mary when it says, "The Holy Spirit, 'The Lord and Giver of Life,' is sent to sanctify the womb of the Virgin Mary and divinely fecundate it, causing her to conceive the eternal Son of the Father in a humanity drawn from her own" (n. 485).

Thus, the clear testimony of the Holy Bible and of the teaching of the Catholic Church is that Jesus has no human father, his 'Father' is Father from all eternity, God Himself. As both perfect God and perfect Man, Jesus Christ reveals the fullness of truth about God and about man. If we want to know how to live as a son or daughter of God, we have to look to Jesus: "I am the way, and the truth, and the life; no one comes to the Father but by me," (John 14:6).

MUSLIM FRIEND: I can see where you are coming from.

ME: So who is the Father of Jesus?

MUSLIM FRIEND: I am not going to say it as I would lose my religion. I see why you say what you say.

ME: I am only showing you that the Qur'an in the case of the Virginal Conception agrees with the Bible and so Muslims and Christians both believe that Mary became pregnant from the Spirit of God. We simply call that spirit the Holy Spirit.

MUSLIM FRIEND: Okay

Was Jesus on the Cross?

ME: On another note, during high school, you used to tease me about Jesus not dying on the Cross. Why does the Qur'an put him on the Cross, to begin with?

MUSLIM FRIEND: He didn't die on the Cross. Judas replaced him on the Cross and people still thought it was Jesus.

ME: So, Jesus was on the Cross?

MUSLIM FRIEND: Yes, but he didn't die.

ME: Sura 4:157 says, *"So also by their blasphemy and their terrible words of slander against Mary, and they're saying: 'It is we who killed the Christ Jesus son of Mary, the messenger of God' – they killed him not, nor did they crucify him, but so it was made to appear to them. Those who disputed concerning him are in doubt over the matter; they have no knowledge thereof but only follow conjecture. Assuredly the killed him not..."*[1] Why is this in the Qur'an?

MUSLIM FRIEND: To show that Jesus didn't die on the Cross.

---

[1] I have taken this quotation from Professor Tarif Khalidi's Penguin Classics translation of the *Qur'an*, 2009 edition, p. 80. For some years Professor Khalidi was Professor of Arabic at Cambridge University, subsequent to which he has held the *Sheik Zayed* Chair of Islamic and Arabic Studies at the American University of Beirut.

ME: This is the only mention of the subject and it comes out of the blue. Why is Jesus on the cross to start with?

MUSLIM FRIEND: He isn't on the Cross, Judas is.

ME: Why would God make it appear to be Jesus even though it was Judas?

MUSLIM FRIEND: To show how the Christians are wrong about the crucifixion.

ME: My question is that since you believe Jesus was on the Cross originally and then Judas replaced Him and it still appeared to be Jesus although it was Judas, why was Jesus put on the Cross in the first place?

MUSLIM FRIEND: I never thought of that

ME: The Qur'an agrees that Jesus appeared to be on the cross. What did He do to deserve that?

MUSLIM FRIEND: I don't know

ME: Historians know that a man named Jesus was on the cross. I won't go into His death but just to be clear he was originally on the cross before Judas right?

MUSLIM FRIEND: Yes

ME: What did Jesus do wrong in the first place to be put on the cross?

MUSLIM FRIEND: Nothing

ME: The reason why Jesus was put on the cross was because according to the Jews He blasphemed by making Himself equal to God. The Jews believed in the one God 'Elohim' and were forbidden to even say His name "I AM" as it would violate their law. Roman history, secular history, Jewish history all agree that a man named Jesus died on a cross even though they don't agree that He was God or the Son of God. This is a historical fact that Jesus died and all because he claimed to be God.

Calling God Father is an Insult to Him

ME : I remember being told in high school that it is an insult to Allah if we call Him Father.

MUSLIM FRIEND: Yes, that's right. If you have a human dad and then call God Father you are putting on Allah human attributes and that is insulting to Him.

ME : If fatherhood was exclusively an earthly thing I can understand that. But as I showed you, Jesus was conceived by the power of the Spirit of God and the only way to bring life into this world is a father and a mother. God is the Father of Jesus.

MUSLIM FRIEND: I told you before that I can see how you got that concept but to call God 'Father' is degrading to Him.

ME: We are not degrading God's name but are lifting ourselves up to Him. God is the first and eternal Father. He is fathering all of us as His children and we as humans don't deserve to be called father but we have the privilege to share in a small way the Fatherhood of God because we can co-create.

MUSLIM FRIEND: Yeah, but the word 'father' came after humans.

ME : Just like every other word we use, but for us to describe who God is we have to understand why we are here. God is Love. God the Father eternally loved God the Son and God the Son eternally loved God the Father in the Holy Spirit, the third person of the Trinity. God was always a Father, before He created us. Jesus in the Bible calls God 'Father' over 175 times.

We ended the debate on friendly terms and kept in touch only casually. He did not become a Christian, but I did leave him with much to think about. I find that with my Muslim friends, when I try to get them thinking about the Holy Trinity, Virginal Conception, birth of Jesus, Crucifixion and the Fatherhood of God, they tend to respond by saying they are forbidden to ask questions outside of the Qur'an because if they do they will lose their religion. I have met dozens of Muslim converts to Christianity over the years and it is great to talk with them. Many come into the Church via a supernatural experience or dream. Everyday I thank God for my Muslim friends.

Next, I want to address a common question posed by many Muslims in regards to Jesus Christ as Son of God.

Where in the Bible does Jesus say "I am God" or "the Son of God, worship me?"

This is a very common question I get from our Muslim friends. I remember the late Ahmed Deedat, a prominent Muslim leader from South Africa who challenged all Christians around the world by saying that he would pay them $1000 if they could find any part of the Bible where Jesus is quoted saying, "I am the son of God, worship me". It is a great challenge and you may initially think that's easy, but what Ahmed Deedat was looking for, along with millions of other Muslims around the world, are the words exactly quoted in that order "I - AM - THE - SON - OF - GOD - WORSHIP - ME". I agree with all Muslims that nowhere in the Bible does Jesus say those exact same words in that exact same order. The problem with this request is that it puts the conditions on God as to how He should reveal His Divine Son. God says it in a much better and convincing way by making sure that the Jews understood what He was claiming. That's why He was crucified, although Islam denies the crucifixion, but that was briefly dealt with in the previous chapter. If we are to be consistent we need to apply the same rules to the Qur'an. Where in the Qur'an does it say the Tawheed? "THERE - IS - ONLY - ONE - GOD

- ALLAH - AND - HIS - PROPHET - MUHAMED". I can make the same claim and offer to pay any muslim in the world $1000 to find in the Qur'an those exact words in that exact order, but that's not the right way to go about these things. Muslims would agree that the Shahada prayer is crucial to the religion of Islam and that every Muslim must recite that prayer if they want to be a Muslim. It is so important to their faith, yet is not in the Qur'an word for word. To be consistent with their logic, they need to change the words to match whatever the Qur'an says. You will find separate parts of that prayer in the Qur'an but not all together in that order.

CHAPTER 6

My Vocation Discernment

Seminary Life, My Wife, Marriage, Children

He who finds a wife finds a good thing,
and obtains favor from the Lord.
(Proverbs 18 : 22)

Seminary Life

So, the day came, on the last Sunday of February 2003, and it was the Opening Mass at the Seminary of the Good Shepherd in Homebush. My whole family came to give me support. It was great! I was shown to my room, which had a single bed, a study desk, a chair and an ensuite, which was nice. We were shown around the place and I must say it was very comfortable and clean. There were thirteen seminarians starting that year, which was the largest group in decades. Cardinal Pell was the main celebrant and hundreds of people came to join in prayer for the seminarians. Over forty-five seminarians were present with their family members. There were people from all over Australia: Queensland, Wollongong, Newcastle, Western Sydney, Lismore and many other interstate visitors. It was a real eye-opener for me to see such a vast range of men from all ages and cultures. There were different factors that led each man to the seminary. I knew why I was there and that was to discern if this was what God wanted of me.

Typical Life in the Seminary

The seminary life was a very well-structured one that involved community meals, prayer and study. A typical day started with the Divine Office Morning Prayer (Lauds) at 6:45am in the chapel, then quiet meditation at 7am followed by Mass at 7:30am. This was all done in the chapel with all the seminarians. We then had breakfast at 8am which was not compulsory, so Paul and I would go for a rosary walk around the block. Paul also joined the seminary which was great, and we would spend lots of time in prayer together. With both of us being Maronites, we were under the Maronite Bishop, while we were studying with the other seminarians. Classes were from 9am until 12pm and lunch was in common and compulsory at 1pm. This was the formal meal of the day and we would often have guests come during this time. Lunch would finish at

1:30pm and then there was free time until 4:30pm when the first-year seminarians would pray the Rosary together in the chapel before Evening Prayer of the Divine Office (Vespers) at 5pm. Dinner followed which was prepared in a buffet style for each seminarian to serve himself, and then evening classes from 6pm until 9pm. After this, we would gather for Night Prayer (Compline) at 9:15pm finishing at 9:30pm. That was the official program from Monday to Friday, with lights out at 10:30pm. I really enjoyed the structure. The discipline was so important, and the day flowed very well. On Saturdays we had free time and Sundays we had Mass together at 9:30am that was open to the public. This was followed by brunch and then an hour of Adoration and Benediction - i.e. adoration of Jesus in the Blessed Sacrament from 5pm to 6pm. I enjoyed my time in the seminary and for the first six months I was really deepening my faith further and my appreciation of the priesthood had grown.

During our mid-year break, my brother Joey and I went on a pilgrimage to Lebanon, organised by the parish of St Joseph's Maronite Church, Croydon. I went a week earlier with Father Bernard and I had such a blessed time. It was my first-ever trip to Lebanon and I gained so much from meeting the different friends of Fr Bernard and watching how he lived out his priesthood. He was very popular and such a prayerful man. I loved to see how the people we met would be so excited to see him. We were going from house to house by foot and would visit up to ten families in the same street. "Abouna!" they would call out and welcome him in for a coffee. They were so hospitable and generous, offering us food and drink and making us feel so welcome. It is commonly known among my non Lebanese friends that the Lebanese hospitality is unlike any other. As true as this may be, we cannot forget where that culture of hospitality comes from. It is rooted in the strong faith that the Lebanese people have in God and their trust in Him during the most horrific times of war and struggle. That is what formed the character of Lebanese Christians.

Father Bernard asked me at one stage whether I wanted to be a married priest, because according to the Maronite Rite, married men can be ordained to the priesthood. I was baptised in the Maronite Rite and therefore had that option. I must say at the time it seemed attractive, as I always wanted to be married. I remember as we would go from house to house, we would be served by the oldest daughter who was still at home. These were very attractive and modest girls who had faith. There was almost an unspoken understanding that seminarians were open to looking for a wife, and any faithful girl would be very happy to marry a man wanting to be a priest. Those who enter the seminary are educated and learn responsibility and become future leaders of a community as a priest. Being served by these very beautiful girls, the thought of marriage entered my mind, and as I asked myself whether one of these Lebanese girls would make a suitable wife for me, I realised I wanted an Australian-Lebanese girl and instantly I thought of Christine. She would be the ideal wife with her faith, generousity and joyfilled nature and I really liked her. From that moment in Lebanon of 2003 the thought of marrying Christine would not leave me and would become the main focus of my prayer and discernment.

After the first week in Lebanon, the rest of the Aussie pilgrims came in time for the two-week pilgrimage. My younger brother joined the group and it was an amazing trip. The group was really close and it almost felt like family very quickly. We would travel all over Lebanon having huge day trips and learning so much about this beautiful culture with so much history. We visited holy sites like St Charbel's Monastery in Anaya, St Rafqa, St Nematallah, Our Lady of Lebanon, Jesus the King, plus Tyre and Sour where Jesus met the Samaritan woman at the well. There were beautiful waterfalls, caves, mountains, beaches, castles made of rock in the mountains, old ruins like Baalbeck and others. The food was so fresh and filling. There was such a huge variety of foods, not to mention the music and social aspect of the culture. I loved to be able to speak to any stranger with the greeting, "God be with you" and "Glory to God" and everyone would respond in Arabic, "Always to God." God was on the tongue of almost everyone and there were statues of saints at the front of everyone's house. We all became good friends from within this group and remain in contact today. There were also a few marriages from the group, which is always good. What a great trip that Lebanon pilgrimage was!

When we returned to Australia, I had difficulty praying without thinking of Christine. She was on my mind constantly as I felt a very strong connection to her. I kept discerning whether it was a temptation to pull me away from the celibate priesthood. I had spiritual direction and continued the studies remaining committed to the seminary in the hope of discerning whether or not I was called to marriage. There was a thirty-day silent retreat at the end of the first year of the seminary. This would have to be one of the times in my life that I found myself closest to God. The thirty-day retreat was based on the spiritual exercises of St Ignatius of Loyola. He describes how prayer can be filled with either consolations or desolation. We can meditate on the life of Christ by putting yourself into the Gospel scenes. Take for example, the birth of Jesus scene.. What was it like? Cold? Smelly? Tiring? Think of how you can help St Joseph with the hay or prepare the crib which was a feeding trough for farm animals. Ask Mary if she needed anything. It is very powerful experience to put yourself in a scene of one of the Gospels and identify with the smallest detail recounted there.

The retreat was completely silent. During mealtimes,

music played in the background. The only time we could talk was in our thirty-minute 'one-on-one' catch-up with our spiritual director and during the responses at Mass. The only three commitments each day were the mealtimes, Mass, and the spiritual direction session. The rest of the day we were free to go for walks or spend time in adoration of the exposed Eucharist or return to our rooms. I had a goal for this retreat, and that was to discern if God was calling me to the priesthood or to marriage, and in particular to Christine. My day would involve praying the seven hours of the Divine Office which we refer to in Latin as: Lauds, Matins, Terce, Sext, None, Vespers and Compline. I also read the book "Story of a Soul" which is the autobiography of St Therese of Lisieux who was also known as 'The Little Flower.' I had a couple of hours of adoration of the Blessed Sacrament each day, meditating on different aspects of the life of Christ and writing down my thoughts during these meditations. I also prayed the four sets of mysteries of the Rosary each day, often doing so on long walks. I would also exercise and listen to talks by Archbishop Fulton Sheen.

I remember doing a five-day prayer novena to St Therese asking specifically about whether I was called to marriage or the priesthood. Although both seemed attractive, I felt strongly about only committing to one at that time. On days eight and twenty-one of the spiritual retreat, we were permitted a day where we could speak, so I called my mum and asked her if she would pray the five-day prayer with me. We said if St Therese provided a white rose then I was called to marriage and if she showed us a red rose it was a calling to the priesthood. I deliberately chose white for marriage as it is much harder to find white roses, so that would be significantly a strong sign. On the last day of the retreat, which also worked out to be the last day of the five-day prayer, the priest asked me if I was any closer to knowing God's Will in my life. I said, "I am not sure as I don't want to turn my back on God if I get married, and how do I know if God is calling me or Satan is distracting me so I don't join the priesthood?" Noticeably frustrated, the priest almost shouted at me saying "Charbel! What do you want?" I said back in a loud voice, "I want Christine!" He smiled and leaned back in his chair and took a breath of relief. He said, "You have your answer," and left the room. I was breathing heavily and looked out the window and then noticed a white rose right there just outside the window! I had not told anyone else about my prayer request except for mum, so it could not have been a set-up. When I got home that day I told my mum what happened. She also had found a white rose in her garden, which was the first time one had ever appeared there. I felt I had received my answer and called the bishop to notify him that I didn't believe that God was calling me to the priesthood. He encouraged me to go to Lebanon for six months to discern further and make sure, as maybe a different setting might change things. So, I did.

Now I had to tell my mother and family that I was going to Lebanon and they organised a farewell for me. I remember saying goodbye to my little brother Joey at the airport and the tears that ran down his face and the strong hug he gave me were pretty emotional. I remember being moved by that and it hit me then that I was stepping out in faith to see if this was God's calling. I had a special bond with my little brother, and I am so proud of the way he has turned out in his faith. The plane trip was a long one and when I arrived in Lebanon the weather was freezing. It was winter and the seminary had ice on the ground. I realised how bad my Arabic was in the first three months of arriving. Paul joined me and we had our own timetable to follow. It was a unique situation since we had to organise our own internal classes, learning Arabic and sitting in theology classes in Arabic and not understanding them. We also had internal lessons on Syriac and some Maronite History. I really enjoyed this experience as well. Around Easter my mother came to visit me and I remember sharing with her how I was still not any clearer about my vocation. We had such a good time travelling around the country and visiting family. We had a break for Easter so it was perfect timing to be with mum.

I remember that when I took mum to the airport, she expressed how much she wanted to support me and hoped that she had helped me clarify my decision. When she could see I was still confused she became emotional

83

and I remember feeling really bad, as I had a strong pull toward marriage but wanted to make sure it was God's Will.

My brother Armando got married to his fiancee Sari in the following month. I was under real pressure to go to the wedding, but the bishop didn't allow me to attend and I was bound to obedience. I knew I had to give the discernment absolutely everything. I missed my brother's wedding for the sake of knowing I gave God everything. In July of that same year I made my decision. I thought it was a good time to make that decision as the bishop was about to send me and Paul to Rome. I actually wanted to go to Rome and this now was my test. As a Maronite seminarian I could get married and the idea of reaching out to Christine and asking her to consider courting while I studied in Rome was crossing my mind and was very attractive to me. As much as I desired to go to Rome however, I had to do what was right and return home. I could not in good conscience continue, knowing that the call to marriage was pretty loud and clear in my mind. I told the bishop I wanted to return home. He accepted my choice and welcomed me back anytime. I actually felt at peace with my decision and that's how I knew it was from God. God gives you peace when you are acting according to His will. The devil comes and goes, while God is always there, and when I think about it, the thought of a vocation to marriage never left me, and that's how I knew it was God's will to marry.

Earlier in this chapter I referred to how in the Maronite Rite of the Catholic Church, married men can be ordained to the priesthood. Across history and right up to the present day, the Maronite Church has produced so many great and holy priests who were married. In the Maronite Rite however, a priest cannot get married after being ordained to the priesthood. Also, all bishops and monks have to be celibate.

While not detracting from the place of married priests in the Maronite Church, I should also mention that the Catholic Church's teaching and discipline on priestly celibacy in the Latin Rite is well-grounded in the words and example of Jesus. It was Jesus himself who first required his apostles to leave wife and family in order to become 'eunuchs' for the sake of the Kingdom of Heaven: "For there are eunuchs who were born that way, and there are eunuchs who have been made eunuchs by others - and there are those who choose to live like eunuchs for the sake of the kingdom of heaven. The one who can accept this should accept it," (Mt 19:12).

In totally committing Himself to the mission he had received from the Father, Jesus chose to live in the celibate state. While married men can be ordained in the Maronite Rite, in the Latin Rite of the Catholic Church, celibacy is mandatory. In praising priestly celibacy for the great fruits of holiness and service it produces in the Church and in the world, the Second Vatican Council said:

> "The Church's holiness is fostered in a special way
> by the manifold counsels which the Lord proposes
> to his disciples in the Gospel for them to observe.
> Towering among these counsels is that precious
> gift of divine grace given to some by the Father (cf.
> Mt 19:11; 1 Cor. 7:7) to devote themselves to God
> alone more easily with an undivided heart (cf. 1
> Cor 7: 32-34) in virginity and celibacy. This perfect
> continence for love of the kingdom of heaven has
> always been held in high esteem by the Church
> as a sign and stimulus of love, and as a singular
> source of spiritual fertility in the world".[2]

While recognising that celibacy "is not demanded of
the priesthood by its nature,"[3] the Second Vatican Council
nevertheless reaffirmed its connection with priestly
ordination when it said:

> "[C]elibacy, which at first was recommended to
> priests, later in the Latin Church imposed by law on
> all who were to be promoted to Holy Orders. This
> legislation, pertaining to those who are destined
> for the priesthood, this holy synod again approves
> and confirms, fully trusting this gift of the Spirit

---

2   Vatican II, *Lumen Gentium*, n. 42

3   Vatican II, *Presbyterorum Ordinis*, n. 16

so fitting for the priesthood of the New Testament, freely given by the Father, provided that those who participate in the priesthood of Christ through the sacrament of Orders-and also the whole Church-humbly and fervently pray for it.–."[4]

My Wife, Marriage, Children

On June 29, 2004 I arrived home. I remember the day vividly. Christine and her friend Ingrid were visiting my mother. I greeted them both and I am pretty sure Christine could see my excitement. I didn't say anything to her that day, but the very next day I sent her a text message inviting her to meet me at the Church of St Michael's in Belfield at 2pm the following day, Thursday July 1, 2004. I arrived at the church and noticed that Christine was already there kneeling and praying. I knelt next to her and we prayed a short prayer to Jesus in the tabernacle. We then went for a walk to the local park, which I used to walk past every morning on my way to primary school. It was called Rudd Park and we sat on a bench and discussed a future together. I asked the most important question of course - "Are you seeing anyone?" - and thankfully Christine responded that she was not! I let her know that I really want to get to know her more closely and she said she would like that. So began my transition from the seminary

---

4   Ibid

to talking to Christine and officially dating (traditionally known as courting) within two days of my return. I felt so blessed and excited as I embarked on this next phase of my life!

I remember the first few months of our dating and courtship which were always fun, joyful, spiritual and fulfilling. Christine would ask questions about future plans, career, hopes, marriage and family ideals, and of course, faith. I had an opportunity to commence working immediately, driving a meat delivery van. This involved organising orders for butchers, loading up a van and delivering the meat across Sydney. It was really enjoyable and I took advantage one day of calling Christine when I had one more delivery to do, asking if she wanted to go for a ride in the meat van. She did! So, I delivered the final drop-off to a butcher and we went for a coffee nearby. That was our first official date and it was in a meat van with some blood on me delivering a quarter of a cow to a butcher. I knew Christine was a keeper after that! I continued working in that job for a couple of months before working full-time with my brother Albert in the landscaping business. It was a way to get back into the workforce right away. I did that for the rest of the year and it was hard work.

In 2005, I enrolled in the Australian College of Physical Education in Homebush, Sydney to study for a Bachelor degree in Personal Development and Physical Education.

It was a three-year degree which qualified me to teach P.E in both primary and secondary schools. Christine had just got a job teaching full time at Tangara School for Girls in Cherrybrook and I did my first practical at Redfield College in Dural. We drove to work together which was great for the three weeks I had to be at Redfield. I also acquired my personal training license and pool lifeguard certificate. I worked again as a gym instructor and lifeguard at the Sydney International Aquatic Centre outside my classes. I was enjoying my time at college and work, knowing it was going to give me the qualifications needed to teach in schools full-time. I must say, the first six months after leaving the seminary were very difficult as I came to terms with how fast the world had progressed and changed since I had entered the seminary. I was not up to date with technology developments, local news, culture and fashions. It felt like I had been lifted off the conveyor belt of life for eighteen months and then put back on and I had to catch up!

Finally, the time arrived for me to meet Christine's family. It was a little intimidating for me meeting Christine's father and her relatives, who seemed quite successful in their careers. I had the hard '-talking--to'- from her dad who told me that I needed a degree or a business. He was nervous for his daughter as he was not sure that I could provide for her. So that first six months was tough and thanks to Christine's understanding and our regular chats, we worked out a plan and managed to be very comfortable with our situation.

In May of 2005 I had registered Parousia Media as a sole trader business and began to offer the St Joseph Communication's CDs to bookshops and friends. (I'll go into that detail in the next chapter when I talk about the Parousia Media journey, but I needed to mention it here to keep things moving chronologically.) On July 1, 2005, I proposed to Christine and she said 'Yes!' I planned a day out for the first year of our courtship and had a letter written for her at various locations. We started at St Charbel's Church where we first met and then drove to Umina Beach, where we had spent time during summer. We then went to the city, before heading back to St Michael's Belfield and Rudd Park down the road. I had my younger brother Joey have a bottle of champagne, flowers, the ring and my letter sitting on the bench where we had our first chat. He was hiding in the car ready to take photos of me on my knee asking Christine to marry me. I read the letter to Christine, then knelt down and popped the question. She teared-up and answered, "Yes". We have photos of that joy-filled day which we cherish. There was a lady walking her dog who came over and congratulated us, which was nice. Later that evening, I organised for my parents to visit Christine's parents so I could ask their blessing. I remember Christine's mother's reaction - she nearly fell off her seat and was very happy for us. So, we were engaged on July 1, 2005 exactly one year to the day from when we started to date.

We then had to organise the wedding as I continued to complete my studies. We were married at St Charbel's on July 1, 2006, and it was also our engagement and dating anniversary. (I must say it's very handy having only one date to remember.) I should also admit that a one-year engagement felt so long for us. We were ready after three months and in the end, although I had not yet finished my studies, we made things work.

The wedding was very special and I got a little emotional as Christine walked down the aisle. We had four-hundred people at our wedding and it was a day to remember. I was the fifth child and it worked out to be the fifth wedding in our family with only Joey remaining single at that time. (He actually discerned a religious vocation himself at one point, but discerned pretty quickly that God was calling him to marriage.) Joey was my Best Man as we spent the most time together being so close in age. We had a Maronite Mass with six priests including Father Chris who was my best friend and the one who had given me all the Scott Hahn tapes. The main celebrant was Father Maroun Azzi who was finishing his seminary studies as I was starting mine, and he was a good mentor during those years. There were Father Peter and Deacon Richard from the seminary, plus Father Eli, Father Peter Joseph and finally Father Tohme who was the monk who baptised and confirmed me. The Mass was so special and St. Charbel's was the perfect church for our wedding. From the day I was born I was not only named Charbel in honour of the great saint, but also baptised and confirmed at St. Charbel's. We attended Sunday Mass there in the early years, I met Christine there and it had been a major part of my life since returning to the Church.

We then went on to the Reception that night in Bankstown's 'La Luna Lounge' and it was a great night. The speeches were very special, and the entertainment was fun. We had the Lebanese drums and the famous dabke music. It was so much fun to see all my family, including the cousins of my parents and lots of relatives we hadn't seen for a while. We also had traditional Colombian dancers on the night and it was so good to celebrate in all three cultures with Lebanese, Colombian and Australian music.

I had my high-school friends at our wedding, including my good Muslim friends. I was grateful that they came and joined in the special day for me. I went down to the dance floor to give my speech, holding my new bride's hand. I wanted everyone to know how special she was and how much of an impact she had on me. She truly made me a better person and that's when you know you have the right match in life. If your spouse brings the best out in you then you are destined for each other. I explained how a wedding is a foreshadowing of the eternal wedding banquet in heaven. The 'Wedding Feast of the Lamb' as we understand it. My wish was to remind people that we are here only for a short time and earthly marriage does not last beyond death into eternity. Marriage in this life helps us prepare for the ultimate and everlasting party in Heaven with God and with all his angels and saints. One prayer I mentioned was a regular prayer that Christine would pray each hour and it was influenced by St Jean Vianney, who blessed each hour of the day with a Hail Mary. We simply added this prayer which is inspired by him. It goes like this:

"Blessed be God. Courage, my Soul
Time passes, Eternity approaches,
Let us live as we hope to die,
Blessed be the Name of the Lord".
(Then you recite one Hail Mary.)

This prayer would be said each hour of the day. We often missed out on it, but we would pray it regularly throughout our day. The night concluded; Christine and I didn't go back to a hotel room, but we spent the wedding night in our newly-owned home in Georges Hall. We had purchased a two-bedroom weatherboard home eleven months previously and had a tenant renting there until a week before we got married. We had a busy time painting, changing carpets and polishing floor boards. We went on our honeymoon to Port Douglas in North Queensland for eight days. It would be the longest getaway we would have together until the present day.

I increased my work load in 2006 and asked to do extra classes so I could finish quicker than normal. I finished my degree in two-and-a-half years. Within three months Christine was pregnant, with our first child. We were worried in those first few months as we were open to life and Christine was not falling pregnant but by the third month we had our blessing. The pregnancy was very smooth until the last month. We had a great doctor who was a family man with eleven children of his own. He noticed the amniotic fluid was low and recommended Christine get induced to make sure the baby was delivered without any complications. It was three weeks early and, after thirty-six hours, our first child was born on May 29, 2007. We named him Michael Anthony Raish and he was so tiny but was healthy, thank God. I remember the first night bringing him home and noticing that for the first time we had another person in the room. It was a profound moment as only a few days earlier he was not born and only eight months earlier he didn't exist. That night, I realised that I was now a father and Christine was a mother. We could not imagine life without this little baby. I think that is such a powerful lesson for us that once life enters into existence you are transformed forever, and this life will live forever as it is a new soul. Michael was baptised on our first wedding anniversary at St Charbel's Church by Fr Bernard, the priest who took me to Lebanon the first time and asked me if I wanted to ever get married. He also had a huge impact on me spiritually. So we now had a fourth anniversary sharing the same date. July 1, 2004 both Christine and I began to date and court each other. July 1, 2005, we got engaged. July 1, 2006, we were married. On July 1, 2007, we baptised our first child. I think you can understand that July 1 is pretty special to us.

At the end of 2007 I graduated from ACPE with a Bachelor's Degree in Personal Development and Physical Education. In 2008, I got my first job, which took me back to my old high school, Belmore Boys. It was so good to be working there and it took a lot of getting used to calling my old teachers by their first name as they were now my work colleagues. I was also working in the Gym at Canterbury Leagues in Belmore and lifeguarding at the Sydney International Aquatic Centre that year. I also enrolled in a Masters of Arts and Theological Studies at the University of Notre Dame in the same year and would complete that in two years. My days were long as I would get up at 6am to train clients at the gym before going to school from 8:30 to 3:30pm, then returning to the gym for the night shift until 10pm. I would repeat this a few times a week. My full-time job was now teaching but I also did lots of hours at the gym and pool. On the weekends I would get up at 4:30am to open up the gym. I did this until the end of that year.

In 2008, our second child was born into the world. Raphael John Raish was born on August 11, 2008, only fourteen months after Michael. Christine was also working full-time as a teacher at Retavale in Belfield, a private infant school that was part of the Tangara School for girls run by the PARED foundation. We were extremely busy that year. In addition to my three jobs and two children, I was also organising talks for Guardians at St Charbel's church. The year 2008 was very important for Sydney as World Youth Day was held there. Just before it started, I got a call from the headmaster of Redfield College offering me a job as a PDHPE teacher starting the next term. I remember declining it at the time as I was really enjoying myself at 'Belmore Boys'. After speaking with my coordinator, he suggested I consider the job at Redfield again, as it better aligned with the purpose for which I had studied, further to which he said the private school system was a good environment to work in. I ended up taking the job and began work as a PDHPE teacher at Redfield College which was a brother school to Tangara. So my wife and I were working for the same organisation: the PARED Foundation.

By the end of 2008 I could not keep up the long drives to Dural from Georges Hall as well as my night shifts so I stopped working at the gym and pool to focus on teaching and my children. Within nineteen months of Raphael's birth we welcomed our third child and this time it was a girl! She was the second girl among the eleven cousins she had at that time. Her name is Elizabeth Mary Raish and she was born on April 8, 2010. Life was extremely busy, and Christine cut right back on work and was just a casual teacher as we now had three children at the age of three and under. Yes, there were three nappies to change and three baby seats squashed in the back seat of our car. Parenting is such a blessing and privilege as we are co-responsible with God for bringing these young ones into the world. Some people can't have children and with years of trying it can be very difficult for a couple in those situations. It is a reminder for me that I didn't deserve one child, let alone three. Christine and I remember those years well and having three young children was the hardest time for us.

The first baby was difficult because of the unknown and learning things for the first time. The second is more difficult because there are now two babies and double the workload. Three at that young age is extremely difficult because now you have triple the workload and very young children totally dependent on you. On November 22, 2011, Gabriel Francis Raish was born, only nineteen months apart from his older sibling again. Because of the increase of difficulty we had had from two to three we were expecting the worst with number four but surprisingly it was not as difficult as expected. Although not any easier, we did notice Michael at the age of four, was just old enough to assist with basic things like putting the nappies in the bin and packing things away. He was also out of nappies himself and could entertain his siblings. We had all four children in the bedroom. Four baby seats, two cots and a double bunk bed.

In 2012, Christine and I were looking to upgrade to a larger home but it was very tight financially for us, now on a single income, especially being a fourth year teacher making mortgage repayments plus all the other expenses. We managed to revalue our home and used the equity to build a granny flat at the back. This assisted with the repayments and increased the value of the home. I was still involved with Guardians, church life, teaching, and running Parousia Media, which was always on the side.

A work colleague of mine, Chris Tanna, approached me about an opportunity to purchase acreage near Redfield College that had two homes. We could purchase it together and share the costs. It meant paying only half of the cost of a property, and after months of negotiating and investigating, and of course praying to St Joseph, we secured a larger home on acreage only twelve minutes away from work. I need to mention my wife's prayers for this intention, a powerful prayer based on listing all your needs for a home on paper. You must be specific and not hold back. Christine and I wanted a place that was big enough to entertain friends and have people visiting our home regularly. We wanted a place big enough to have a room dedicated to homeschooling. Acreage was also a dream along with a classic-look home not too fancy but clean and comfortable with plenty of space. Christine even wrote down that she wanted the corners of the ceiling to be beautiful which I thought was a little overboard. She sent this letter to nuns in France who pray to St Joseph for your intentions. Within months of that process, came this opportunity along with the price for the exact amount of which we could get approval! St Joseph came through for us and so our next child was named in honour of St Joseph.

On February 4, 2014, our fifth child was born, and yes, we had another boy. We named him Joseph Peter Raish and he was our first child in this new home. We now had room to homeschool and have people over and still have space. Joseph Peter was baptised on the Feast of the Chair of St Peter by a good priest and friend of ours, Father Peter Joseph. The godfather was my brother Joseph but he was unable to make it to the baptism so we had Christine's brother-in-law Peter as the proxy. The beautiful symbolism that this all had for us was not planned at all. We now had five children in the space of six years and were really growing as a family thanks be to God. The three older children were helping out more with chores at home and being home-schooled they became regular helpers for us.

Our sixth child was born on September 13, 2016 -

another boy - which meant we now had five boys and one girl. We named him Benedict Chrysostom Raish and the nice thing about this was that my friend, Father Chris, is a Benedictine monk who took on the religious name of Chris after St John Chrysostom. He was happy to hear the news about our son's name. Benedict was a handful, to say the least, but, thank God, healthy like the others. He is very dark-skinned and noticeably has the strong Colombian features, unlike the other children. Our seventh child Catherine Marie Petra Raish who was born on April the 24th, 2018. Christine and I wanted to give a middle name with some variation of Mary to any girl we had, so we gave this baby the name Marie as Elizabeth took the name Mary. There is a third name given and that is Petra which is in honour of Christine's late cousin Pierre Haddad who had passed away only one year previously.

So, that's a quick look at my own family journey with Christine and having seven children in eleven years. I certainly found my vocation and calling as a husband and father. Each time a child is born that vocation gets strengthened. I am truly blessed to have a large family and I am still learning how to be a better father and husband. This is a journey for all of us and it is one that both Christine and I know we can't do without God. We still homeschool all the children and we try to get to Mass a few times a week as a family. We aim to pray the Rosary each night together - it happens most days. We also have

Night Prayer together where we line up facing the icons of Jesus and Mary that were painted by Father Chris and it includes an Examination of Conscience. We all kneel and have a minute's silence thinking of our day, then say an Act of Contrition before I bless each child with holy water and send them to bed. I love family life and, thanks be to God it gets better and better each day. Having a large family may not be easy but it is so fulfilling, and I must say that the good times far outweigh the tough times. I could write a whole book on family life but I want to keep things moving and I will now dedicate the next chapter to my other vocation-with-a-small 'v', which is my ministry, Parousia Media. Let's go back to 2005 and see how this ministry began and what it looks like today.

CHAPTER 7

Parousia Media Began:
I Found My Calling

Evangelisation, Formation, Leadership

Go therefore and make disciples of all nations,
baptising them in the Name of the
Father and of the Son and of the Holy Spirit.
(Matt 28 : 19)

I need to go back to 2004, when I came back from the seminary and wanted to get more Scott Hahn cassettes from Father Chris. He said the local distributor at the time had retired and the technology had changed to CDs. So I contacted the supplier in America - St Joseph Communications - in West Covina, California. A man named Ruben Quezada answered and he was such a friendly voice on the phone. He took my order for some Scott Hahn CDs but, when it came to the shipping, the freight cost was more than the cost of the products themselves. Actually, it was about three times as much. I asked him if there was a more affordable way of getting the CDs and he suggested to manufacture them locally, which would eliminate the shipping. They had a process at the time to allow international distributors to license the materials and pay a 10% royalty. I asked him what I needed to do, and he informed me that I needed to establish a website, come up with a trading name and select the master copies needed. I needed time to think about this, as that would require a bit of commitment.

At that time, I was talking with my friend from the seminary, Father James Foster, who had the idea of having a one-stop shop of Catholic Faith formation resources. He set up a meeting with Anthony Cleary, who was the director of the CCD (Confraternity of Christian Doctrine), an agency aimed at forming the Catholic student in public schools. There was a bookshop as part of the agency, and so we thought it would be good to expand the range. I mentioned that I had just acquired information from St Joseph Communications which would allow me to license the materials. I offered to assist the CCD in setting this up and they could be the distributor, but Anthony insisted that since it was my idea initially I should pursue it myself.

I did not know how to build a website, so I contacted a good friend of mine, Anthony Succar, who is a quadriplegic, but an expert in coding websites. We sat down together for hours coming up with a name. We wanted either a Latin, a Greek or Hebrew name that reflected the Second Coming of Christ. After looking at Latin and Hebrew we then came across a Greek name, 'Parousia'. After doing a search we found only one music group that was called by that name. There was no Catholic apostolate with that name so we registered the website www.parousiamedia.com and on May 10, 2005 ,'Parousia Media' the trading name, was born. Now that we had registered the name and had a web address, I placed my first order with St Joseph Communications, which was for twenty Scott Hahn products. I found a company in Silverwater, Sydney, that would replicate CDs. For only a few dollars per CD we reproduced the sets. I had ten of each title made initially and then had them in a box that lived in the boot of my car. The first customer was Anthony Cleary from the CCD who purchased two of each title. We were underway and I had made my first sale. In 2005, I was studying my teaching degree and would monitor the website in between classes. If someone needed a receipt, I would create a basic excel invoice. The word spread slowly and bookshops started to contact me wanting Scott Hahn CDs. The twenty titles were uploaded to the website and as people requested a title from St Joseph Communications I would order them next. The list of titles grew organically from twenty to two hundred in the first 4 years.

2009 - Tim Staples
Our First Ever Tour

After the 2008 World Youth Day, there were a good number of initiatives born in the Church of Australia. In 2009, I wanted to get Scott Hahn out to Australia, but it proved to be difficult and he was not able to come at that time. So, the next speaker in line who had the largest range of CDs was Tim Staples. The tour was creating such a splash in Sydney and word was spreading fast about how dynamic and knowledgeable Tim Staples was. Over 6,000 people turned up over the seven days of talks in Sydney. The week included sixteen talks that were all free to attend and we covered costs by way of donations from passing buckets around after the talks. We raised enough money to cover all the costs and had enough left over to pay for the airfares for the next tour.

Before I talk about the other tours, I want to mention some of the comments from that week with Tim Staples. Many people came who were sitting on the proverbial fence with their faith. After hearing Tim they would say that they were convinced the Catholic Church was the One True Church. Others were not Catholic at all but said the points he made were making sense and they would investigate further. Others were so motivated to spread the faith they began their own initiatives. There was a huge reawakening of the faith and the impact was felt across the city and in fact word spread across the country.

2010 - Fr Mitch Pacwa, Steve Ray & Alex Jones
Our Second Tour

In 2010, we wanted to organise another tour. It was a Facebook message from Steve Ray, who heard of Tim's visit, that stimulated an invitation for him to come to Australia. We also wanted Deacon Alex Jones who was a former Pentecostal Minister and has since passed away. The other speaker was Father Mitch Pacwa, who was very knowledgeable on a range of topics and we really wanted him also. We did not intend to get all three at once but what happened was that I sent an email to Alex Jones first but did not hear from him for two weeks so I then pursued Steve Ray, which again took a while, then Father Mitch, and so a whole month went by with no real answer from any of the speakers. We were getting worried and were preparing for a fourth option but overnight the three of them responded and all agreed to come out! We had a decision to make - should we bring all three out or just one? Thankfully, they were open to negotiating a smaller stipend each and this allowed us to bring all three, so we did.

In July of 2010, the Fullness of Truth tour was launched; and we had all three speakers come to Australia.

We expanded to four other cities outside of Sydney making five in total. The tour lasted twenty days with Alex Jones and Steve Ray arriving during the first ten days and then tag teaming with Father Mitch who would stay for another ten days. Over forty talks were given across five cities and twenty consecutive days to over ten thousand people. Praise God, this work was spreading and thousands of people were getting fired up in their faith. Again so many people were excited and recharged in their faith. We also filmed the talks and produced DVDs to make them available for purchase. The range for Parousia Media was growing as a result and the number of partners was growing too. I was still working full-time at Redfield College teaching PDHPE while spending my spare time organising the events and fulfilling orders for Parousia Media. I must thank the core team of volunteers who worked tirelessly during these first two tours - Khalil, Charbel, Anthony and Michael.

2011 - My USA trip and six tours spread
across the year
Our Third Year of Events

In 2011 we decided it would be better to spread speakers across the year, as it was too difficult to manage non-stop events for almost a month. I took the leap of faith and cut back to part time work at Redfield College. I worked as a teacher for three days a week and on Parousia Media for two days a week. I also employed my first staff member, Annie, who helped with answering phone calls and packing orders. I moved out of the garage and shared a shop with my brother Philip. He established a printing business called WildFX and found a shop front in Revesby Sydney. It was great to have more room and a place for customers to walk into. This particular year we had 5 speakers: The Human Experience team, Father Fortea, Jason Evert, Tim Staples and Raymond De Souza along with a few bonus talks with John Pridmore. Before I describe these tours briefly, I want to describe my trip to the United States of America in 2011.

I knew I wanted to expand Parousia Media further. To make things sustainable I needed to partner with more providers and have strong relationships with the speakers. I had to pick the school holidays to travel, and so January was a quiet time of year. There was a West Coast Biblical conference organised by St Joseph Communications with Dr Scott Hahn, Dr Brant Pitre and Dr Michael Barber. I arrived in Los Angeles and slept the first night in the offices of St Joseph Communications in West Covina. I hired a car from the airport with a navigator, and set out to drive in a foreign country for the first time, and on my own. The cars drove on the wrong side of the road and I remember my first turn out of the hire car shop I was on the wrong side and an approaching car put me back on track pretty quickly. The hardest thing actually was positioning the car inside the lanes, as the steering wheel was also on the opposite side of the car, which gives you a different experience when driving.

I got to meet Terry Barber for the first time, who is the founder of St Joseph Communications, and met Ruben, who had answered the phone only six years earlier, along with some other well-known speakers. The Thursday I arrived was spent with St Joseph Communications. On Friday morning I drove out to San Diego to meet the Catholic Answers team. Tim Staples had organised for Karl Keating, Jimmy Akin, Patrick Coffin and some admin executives to join us in this two-hour meeting. It was great to see them all and Karl simply asked me, "What can we do for you?" I explained my desire to partner with Catholic Answers for Australia in regards to resources and speakers. It went well and was promising but it would take a further three years before the partnership would eventually become official. We had lunch together and then I rushed back to Los Angeles to be there at the opening dinner for the conference.

I managed to see Scott Hahn. I walked up to him to greet him and he was happy to know I came from Australia. This encounter was interrupted and so it was a brief thirty seconds together and I thought I had lost my chance to chat with him. Later that night I was tapped on the shoulder; it was Scott Hahn, who said he was intrigued as to why I would come all the way from Australia for this conference. So, I told him about the apostolate Parousia Media and he immediately recognised the meaning of the word as he would talk about the Parousia often in his talks. I also added that we really would love for him to come to Australia and he said he would love to at some point but was not sure when. He gave me his private email address and we kept in touch. I would again see Scott throughout the conference which was great.

After Los Angeles, I continued my journey. It was time to visit the Eternal Word Television Network (EWTN). I was picked up from Birmingham airport by Father Mitch Pacwa and he welcomed me into his home which is right at the network. Father Mitch established an apostolate called Ignatius Productions and so I was able to visit his team and see his office and thereby establish our partnership. Father also showed me around the EWTN studios and set up some meetings with key people there. I also met with Michael Warsaw and Doug Keck to discuss partnering for the home videos. Thanks be to God, they were happy to give us the license to reproduce the DVDs in Australia and pay them a royalty. I sat in some live shows and was able to visit the amazing Shrine of the Blessed Sacrament at Hanceville, which is where Mother Angelica was staying. I could not meet her, but I was amazed by her vision, boldness and extreme trust in the Lord.

The trip continued on to the East Coast, where my good friend, Raymond De Souza lived. I met the whole family for the first time and stayed as a guest in his home. It was so good to meet them all and we had some great discussions about the mission and the projects he was working on. I also saw the great work of his son Dominic, and was impressed with his design work and creativity. Raymond hinted that his son was looking for work and so I had a little chat and we agreed to work out something. (Dominic stayed at our place in Sydney after this trip and worked for us; he would run the office by answering calls, emails, producing the CDs and DVDs along with doing some design work. By that time, Annie had moved on and we needed someone, so Dominic was the perfect fit for the job.) The US trip continued on to Miami where I met my cousins from my paternal grandmother's side and that was good fun. After spending the weekend there I returned home via Los Angeles and that ended my ten day adventure to the States.

February came and I would return to school to start the teaching year and prepare for our first tour with the Grassroots Films crew who created the documentary '*The Human Experience*'. The tour was in partnership with the Australian Catholic University and so we had screenings of the film across all six campuses as well as some parishes and even movie cinemas. At the conclusion of the first tour, we estimated over four thousand people had seen the movie and heard two of the filmmakers answer questions about their work. *The Human Experience* film is a documentary about two brothers living on the streets of New York with the homeless. They ask them questions like, "What are you living for?", "Why do you get up in the morning?", "What's your purpose in life?" Most of the answers pointed to God and the homeless actually were not wanting anyone to feel sorry for them. The film shows the main character share his experiences of not seeing his father for so many years and so there is a scene at the end that really takes you by surprise - I won't say more about it, but you must see the film.

As you can see the events were growing and the expectation was there that we would keep bringing out speakers. One interesting story was with our next speaker Fr Jose Antonio Fortea, an exorcist from Spain. This tour was an interesting time for me and although I always knew about the Devil it was during this tour that I experienced things that would confirm he is real. On multiple occasions I witnessed people experiencing demonic oppression, which is different from possession. During this tour, we learnt that there are three levels of demonic influence and if we are aware of them we can be ready to fight them. The first level is temptation and this happens to all of us every day of our lives. The second level is oppression; this is when the demons are trying to torment you or scare you from outside and this can lead to a feeling of darkness and emptiness as well, which I experienced. The third is demonic possession, which is having a demon possess your body. This requires an exorcist to bless you and pray over you to expel the demon. Father wanted everyone to make sure they were not afraid of demons as they are not God and so we should not insult God by being scared of them. God is the all powerful One and will protect us. He emphasised that we should be calling on the good angels and saints not the bad angels and then we should be okay.

I'd like to share an incident early on in Father Fortea's visit which involved a friend of mine. About a week before Father Fortea arrived my friend called me to say his neighbour's wife was involved in tarot card reading and some weird things were starting to happen. He explained how the wife was becoming aggressive to the children and losing her temper very easily. She would insult the image of Our Lady and cut up her rosary beads. On one occasion she ran off over the other neighbour's fence, and her husband chased her. When the husband finally caught her, she said, in a man's voice, "Get off me," and threw him off. This really scared the husband, so he asked my friend for help. Multiple priests were asked to come and bless the house but none of them were available. During this time of looking for a priest the husband could not sleep at night. He was hearing his name being called at night. He would hear whispers, scratching, door-knocking, pressure on the chest and other things. He was experiencing demonic oppression. It was as though the demons moved in to torment him at night ever since he got the priests involved. One night, after a few weeks of not sleeping, a priest finally came to bless the house and it was the first night's sleep the husband had. My friend then began to share what was happening to him.

Just when he thought that the husband was doing well, the very same symptoms started happening to my friend. There would be a knock at the door and when he answered the door there was no one to be seen. His name would be shouted from outside but he would not see anyone there. There were footsteps at night, scratching walls, whispers in his ears and even the pressure on the chest, almost like someone was holding him down. There was also a time in that very week when he called me, that his mobile phone was flung from the coffee table. He would put the phone on the table again and when he turned around the phone would be flung on its own; like a demon flicking the phone. Finally the last weird thing that happened to my friend was that on more than one occasion, the house alarm would go off when he had friends over to pray the Rosary for the neighbours, just as soon as they would make the Sign of the Cross. The alarm was connected to a security base who would send an officer to come out to see if everything was ok. The alarm was reset and they tried to pray again. Just as they started making the Sign of the Cross, the alarm went off again. It was almost as though the demons did not want them to pray and did whatever they could to stop them. So not only was my friend's neighbour and then her husband affected, but now my friend himself was experiencing these same torments. So, we organised for Father Fortea to come over to my friend's neighbour's house to bless it.

The day Father Fortea arrived in Sydney, we organised dinner at a local restaurant to inform him what was going on. Only a few days before Father arrived in Australia my friend's neighbour, who was into tarot card reading, came back home after being away for a few weeks. She came back as though nothing happened and seemed very normal. This scared my friend as it was only a few weeks earlier she had that deep masculine voice and extraordinary strength with so much anger. We informed Father of this and he said that the demons can sometimes hide when a priest is coming over. We finished dinner and went over to the house where the husband and wife and my friend were present. Father offered to give them each a blessing, so we went outside for individual blessings. He blessed the wife first, who started saying, "What is going on? I can't feel my legs, I am scared, what's happening?" Father was silently praying over her when she looked like she had fainted and fell to the ground asleep. Father was not worried about her and moved on to my friend to bless him and my friend's right arm started to swing, and he looked a little weak in the legs, but Father supported him, so he didn't fall. My friend opened his eyes and ran to me saying, "Wow, what was that!" He felt a warm charge going through his body and he could not deny its power. Then Father blessed the husband and me, but neither of us felt anything. So, we went inside to understand what just happened. The wife was still on the floor during this time.

Being so confused, we asked Father to help us understand. He told us not to worry about the wife as she was not possessed. The husband then asked why it was that he didn't feel anything during the blessing, so Father offered to bless him again, and this time it was in the lounge room. I was right next to him while the blessing was taking place, and several times Father would ask him if he could feel anything, but there was nothing. Father prayed in Latin, followed by the same question but still the husband was not feeling anything. Then Father began to pray in what sounded like Hebrew, and with his arms he was waving away what could be imagined as smoke, however there was no smoke. Again, Father asked the husband twice if he felt anything, and twice he did not respond. Then, as his eyes were closed, I noticed them flickering as though the eyeballs were rolling around underneath. Father pointed this out to me as the flickering of the eyes continued, and I kept praying my Hail Mary's. Father shouted in a loud voice and in English, "In the Name of Jesus leave this man." He repeated it three times and then the husband fell to the ground and started to shake almost like having a seizure. I am told this had never happened to him before. Then Father prayed over his chest and he calmed down and fell asleep. By this time the wife had awakened and come in from outside to see her husband on the floor. Father blessed her one more time and nothing happened, confirming that she was okay. When the husband woke up, Father told him to read the Bible every day as it is God's Word to us. He told him to go to the church and visit the Blessed Sacrament every day if he could and be around joyous people of faith. Father thanked everyone and I took him to his accommodation.

That night was an eye-opener for me and although I had heard of these things happening to other people, I had never personally witnessed such a thing in my life. For the rest of the tour Father would give his presentation and answer questions before spending time to bless people individually. One friend claimed to have had a healing from blindness while dozens of people fell to the ground while they were being blessed. I counted over twenty people who came up to me sharing the same symptoms as my friend and his neighbour had been experiencing at night. The whispers of their name, scratching, footsteps, knocks at the door and some had pressure on the chest and even some would see a black shadow as an outline of a person. This trip had so many people who had some sort of demonic experience. Some even had suicidal thoughts and could not explain what was going on. There would be one more occasion when there was a minor exorcism in Brisbane and that involved a person shouting aloud while being blessed and falling to the floor. Overall the tour was an eye opener and with over five thousand people being touched I could see the continued impact of this work.

2011 was a big year for us with over 20, 000 people being reached across five cities and six tours. Since then, many other speakers have come; like Jason Evert from The Chastity Project; John Pridmore, the author of *Gangland to Promised Land*, Bishop Barron, Christina King, Leah Darrow, the Dynamic Deacon Harold, Hector Molina, Chris Stefanick and more.

By 2013, Parousia Media had been getting its name around the country with eighteen tours, two hundred events organised and 150, 000 people coming through the doors to hear these powerful speakers. I thought we were going to have another strong year. The hard thing now was that I had to pay wages for a full-time employee - Monica Collits, then Simon Carrington - and the stock was growing as well. The finances were very tight, and I was juggling teaching and running Parousia Media while the family was growing. We pushed through to finish the year with Chris Stefanick, who would speak in Sydney and Melbourne. He was not only hard-hitting but also very entertaining. He was able to play the electric guitar and communicate to a range of audiences as well. He was a great speaker for the youth as well as adults. This was the first time I met Chris and I was very impressed. He had a strong impact on the audience and inspired thousands who came to hear him. He was here for seven days giving over twelve talks in three cities. I remember we filmed a couple of his short video clips for his You Tube channel which was growing in popularity. I filmed the video about mercy; it was filmed at Bondi Beach in Sydney and also showcased at the Poland World Youth Day. The other short clip was filmed by my colleague Victor who was based in Melbourne, which is in front of the famous wall filled with graffiti all over it. Another great production! Chris did very well and reached over four thousand people in his time here.

That was my first nine years with Parousia and I want to mention here the struggle my wife and I had. Since it was growing, which was great, the wages and expenses were also growing. The way Parousia survived was simply by passing buckets around after the talks and selling the resource materials. Sometimes we would find a sponsor to cover some of the tour costs. I was not taking a wage, but it consumed most of my time. Christine and I were expecting our fifth child and we had just moved to our current home which meant our mortgage increased and the finances were very tight. I had to move the office out of Revesby and into my lounge room as I could not pay for the rent. I opened up to Chris Stefanick about this and shared with him that I was contemplating a full-time return to teaching as I couldn't sustain Parousia anymore.

Chris had just switched to speaking full time himself for his apostolate called 'Real Life Catholic' and he had had to make that leap of faith, leaving an Archdiocesan role to become independent. He strongly made the point that we need more people doing this work. Very few people commit to this work full-time and so he encouraged me to stay. I felt comfortable enough to share that with Chris and it was great he could share his experience with me. About a month later, he sent me an email simply encouraging me to not give up and keep going with Parousia Media. I thought that was interesting because I had just approached the headmaster at Redfield College to see if there was a full-time position for me. There was and I returned to full-time teaching while trying to keep Parousia afloat with the help of Simon Carrington. Christine and I were expecting our fifth child and we had to see what we should do in regard to living off a part time salary and dipping in the little that we had to sustain Parousia. We made the decision to go back to full-time teaching which began in 2014.

Before I go on to 2014 I should mention that at the end of 2013 there was a fundraiser for the Philippines run by the Maronite Church. Over eight hundred people were there and I recognised so many that night. I lost count of how many people came up to me to encourage me to keep going with the mission of Parousia even though they did not know about me discerning to possibly give it up due to financial strains. Dozens of people shared with me that the CDs we distributed changed their lives and what an amazing impact they have had on them. Because of the number of people that gave me this overwhelming feedback and the words, "Don't give up, keep going," I could not help but think that God was trying to tell me something.

2014 - New Chapter - Rebirth with a New Partner from Melbourne

It was January 24 and I was home praying to God, saying, "If Scott Hahn agrees to come to Australia then I'll take that as a sign that You want me to continue the work of Parousia Media." I had been pursuing Scott Hahn for years to come here, and although he did not decline the offer, he never really could commit either. So, I thought that if I could make the effort to organise a Scott Hahn conference, then it could possibly be my last event or trigger more events. The very next day I received a phone call from a man named Kevin Bailey. He said he had just come back from a pilgrimage with Scott Hahn in the Holy Land. He mentioned that he asked Scott Hahn to come to Australia and Scott pointed him to me. Kevin said that Scott Hahn told him that if Kevin worked with Parousia Media then he would agree to come to Australia. Kevin asked me what it would take to get him here and we set up a meeting to discuss it. He had no idea of my personal prayer to God the day before. I took that as the third sign I needed, to confirm that God wanted me to continue. It was staff week for Redfield; so I had just returned to full-time teaching, so God didn't waste any time with me.

Now that I had been given the sign to continue, I needed to see how this was going to work. I put it back on God and said in prayer, "Lord, you wanted me to do this, now please show me how this is going to be funded". That very week I got the first of three signs that would confirm how God would provide, and so it began with Week 1 of Term 1. The primary school photocopier broke down. This was a very busy time for the school since teachers are printing workbooks to give out. The company that looked after the copier could not replace the machine for two weeks and so the teachers were desperate. I offered my printer which was still on a lease with two years to go. If the school paid for the lease I could bring the machine right away and so they wanted it right away. Why is this significant? The machine cost me over $1,000 per month to run and having the school take on the lease saved me all that money. I was still able to print our covers when needed but that was it, so the savings were very significant. I thanked God that week, it was a win-win for both the school and me.

I was in charge of the video studio that year at Redfield and I noticed the studio was only being used once a week for an hour. I was thinking to myself it could be a good space for me to move the CDs and DVDs from out of my lounge room. I asked the headmaster at the time if I could set up a Parousia office in the studio at the school and he said it was not going to work as it could be seen as a conflict of interest. Christine and I we were expecting our fifth child the very next week. I was hoping to clear up the lounge room so I could have family discussions there since the family was growing. We had our fifth child on February 4 and named him Joseph after the great saint himself. The next month my wife suggested I pray to St Joseph and ask for his intercession to help Parousia Media. I remember praying in general for Parousia but this time I said a nine-day novena to St Joseph for the intention that God would provide for Parousia Media. The first day of this novena, the headmaster approached me and said he mentioned the proposition to the formation committee about having Parousia Media set up an office in the studio room and they all agreed that it was beneficial for the parents. He told me to me feel free to move in anytime. So, that weekend, my neighbour helped both Simon and me to move all of the shelves and stock from my lounge room into the video studio. I thanked St Joseph for his intercession as God had answered his prayers. This was the second sign and way that God was providing for Parousia. Although He was not giving the ministry money, He was taking away expenses, so with the offices we did not have to pay for a lease or electricity, water, computers, furniture, or even cleaning. Having this space was a big step up from my lounge room and it saved us money at the same time. Being part of the school meant the parents could pop in and purchase stock, so it was like having a shop as well. I also got my lounge room back and this was great for family life.

The very next month God provided once again and this time in the form of a website. I had needed to update our website since it was very old and dated. I researched the best ecommerce websites and did comparisons. The top two at that time were Shopify and BigCommerce. I looked to see if there was a Sydney office for either of them as I wanted to sit down with someone to set it up. BigCommerce had an office in the city so that was the first I pursued. I went to their office downtown and spoke with the sales person there. He showed me around the office; and it was very impressive, as there were over 150 staff working there, and that was just the Sydney office. They had an American base with over 250 staff and were growing from strength to strength. I made eye-contact with a man appearing to be the Senior Manager, who had his own office. He looked familiar but I could not remember where I might have seen him. I asked the sales rep who that man was in the office, and was told that he was the CEO and founder of the company. I just took a chance and said, 'Could you ask him if we ever met?' The sales rep said he was busy at that time but would get back to me. I left the office with a positive experience and looked further into BigCommerce as a platform. The next day I received an email from the sales rep, and he said that the CEO was familiar with me and my work and wanted to offer me six months subscription for free. That was a great deal and I made the choice to join BigCommerce of course.

Before the six-month trial was over I wanted to go in the office again to thank the CEO for his generosity. I was fortunate enough to see him and he asked me to share my story. So, I began to share with him how I got back into my faith and felt a need to evangelise through this ministry of Parousia Media. He shared with me that he actually had attended one of our events and was impacted in a positive way. He encouraged me to keep going with the mission and called in his assistant. He told the assistant to put Parousia Media on our enterprise package at no cost indefinitely. This was a $1,500 per month package and both the assistant and I were blown away. I thanked the CEO and invited him to keep in touch which he was happy to do. The assistant walked me out and said "I don't know what you said but he has never offered that to anybody." I took that as another sign from God and we now had the basic means to at least keep Parousia alive and servicing the needs of those who would contact us.

In late April, Kevin Bailey - the man from Melbourne who wanted to talk about a Scott Hahn tour - was visiting Sydney. He came to visit me at my new office. It was perfect timing as we had just finished setting up the new office with all the shelves and resources. He had never seen anything like it as we had over one thousand different titles on Catholic faith formation. We sat down to discuss the details of a potential national conference with Scott Hahn and Kevin made an offer to assist me if I ever needed help. I thanked him for his time and exchanged emails and contacts to keep in touch. That day I wrote down a wish list of my vision for Australia which included some of the following: (1) Lighthouse Catholic Media kiosks filled with CDs and booklets to be in every parish of Australia. (2) Faith formation nights in every parish that involved each parish hosting a guest speaker each month. (3) Bible-study groups to be rolled out in every parish and weekly prayer evenings in each parish. (4) Free online resources for anyone to download along with radio, television and internet platforms to air local Catholic news. I costed this list to over $1,000,000 and emailed it to Kevin.

About two weeks later Kevin called me to thank me for my email and suggested to partner with me. I was curious as to what he meant and so he went on to say, "Instead of giving you a donation, what about we work out what the ministry is valued at in the sense of goodwill and I can put in some cash as capital and we become equal directors?"

It was only three months ago that I had been considering passing Parousia onto someone, so I had nothing to lose. I spoke with my wife and Kevin came to Sydney the following month to see Raymond De Souza, who was giving talks in May that year. My wife agreed, so Kevin with his wife Grace and I with my wife Christine, set up Parousia Media as a proprietary limited company and were 50% owners of the updated entity. God had now provided to keep Parousia afloat.

2014 had three speakers passing through; Raymond De Souza, Matthew Arnold and Leah Darrow. We had organised a handful of events while I was full-time teaching. On July 1, 2014 (Another 1st of July Anniversary!) Kevin and I had officially become partners, so one of the first things we did was to travel to the United States so he could see the other Catholic apostolates.

I set up some meetings in the USA during the school break between September and October. We landed in San Francisco, where the first meeting was with Father Fessio and Mark Brumley from Ignatius Press. We were invited to join the staff for Divine Office and Holy Mass and to my surprise the translation they used was the same exact way that Father Chris would offer. I felt at home among the staff at Ignatius Press. We had a very blessed meeting and we partnered with Ignatius Press as a result of that meeting as a distributor while for some titles, we signed a license agreement. We then traveled to Los Angeles to see the St Joseph's Communications office, Matthew Arnold and meet with Deacon Harold. From LA we drove down to San Diego to meet the staff of Catholic Answers and, thanks be to God, after five years we finally established a partnership. From San Francisco we travelled to Birmingham Alabama to visit the EWTN studios and it was great to show Kevin around the studios and meet the staff there. Meeting Father Pacwa is always a highlight and we also got to see Edwin Lopez the Asia Pacific manager, Doug Keck and Michael Warsaw. That was a good two days spent and great introduction for Kevin.

We then travelled up to Chicago and paid a visit to the staff at Lighthouse Catholic Media. We were blessed not only to see Mark Middendorp and Tim Truckenberg but also Father Michael Gaitley, who gave us a powerful talk. The relationship with Lighthouse only strengthened as a result and we continued to promote the transforming CDs. From Chicago we drove by Mundelein Seminary - at that time, Bishop Barron was the rector- and also spent time with Christina King and her family. From Chicago we went to Philadelphia to visit both the Theology of the Body Institute and Ascension Press. We established a partnership with Ascension Press as a result of this visit. From Philadelphia, Kevin and I drove across the states to Steubenville and stayed with Scott and Kimberly Hahn for two days. It was so good to see Scott Hahn again and to spend time with the family. Scott showed us around the Franciscan University and also the office of the St Paul Centre. Scott asked me how things were going with Kevin as he felt responsible to a degree for our relationship. I said it was going very well and was so confident God wanted this partnership. From Pittsburgh airport we returned home via San Francisco. That was our whirlwind trip around the States in ten days.

2015 - Tim Staples, Deacon Harold
Philippines and Our First Fundraiser Dinner

In 2015 I returned to part time teaching as a result of this new partnership with Kevin. This allowed me to focus on growth and outreach. We needed to develop a proper business plan and budget as well as finding the staff to support this mission. So, I began to get some more help with the mission finding an admin assistant and some volunteers. We tried to set up systems and put them in place. Thanks to Victor, Sam, Simon, Maryanne, and mum, of course, we started to see what was needed to improve our processes and reach as an apostolate. I was watching so many You Tube videos on business planning and motivational talks on leadership and making a difference. We realised it was going to be tough just relying on $5 CDs to make ends meet. We needed a fundraiser and we used the opportunity with the Tim Staples visit to organise one. Tim visited with his wife Valerie that year and gave ten talks over seven days. Tim Staples was as good as ever and this time he was not only quoting the Bible and Catechism by heart but also papal encyclicals and other church documents. We had over four thousand people reached in seven days and also had over four hundred people for our first ever fundraiser dinner with Tim Staples as our keynote speaker. Thanks be to God, we raised enough funds to hire a much-needed production manager who would be responsible for getting the stock ready and take orders at the time. Our first ever full-time staff member. We employed Mark Griffin who came straight from Church Store Supplies and that was great preparation for this role as he had to deal with so many items. The dinner would not have been as successful as it was without the help of my good friend Salwa Elias and she stayed on at that time to be my personal assistant and administrator.

This dinner was our first real milestone since the partnership with Kevin and it was great to see so many people wanting to support us. The next tour was the Dynamic Deacon, and this was his third visit as well, just like Tim. His tour was also great, reaching five thousand people over ten days in Australia followed by another eight days in the Philippines. It was the first-ever overseas Parousia tour. Deacon spoke to over seven thousand people in the eight days as he was giving homilies, talks in packed churches and travelling all over Manila through the very heavy traffic. We covered so much ground, and although financially the tour was not very fruitful, there was no taking away the great impact Deacon had spiritually on those who turned up. Later that same year Deacon would go to Singapore and Kevin and I would support him there as well. So now we had our second international tour and met more people in the Asia Pacific region. There was a quick meeting in Kuala Lumpur during this time to see if Parousia could work with people there in expanding the reach of this ministry. We established some good contacts and are now working with NAC Publications for all our book printing. After the Singapore trip I had to come straight to Adelaide to support Jason Evert for the Australian Catholic Youth Festival where we had over three thousand young people. I noticed the increase of activity in travel and outreach and the name was getting more known.

2016 was the year I switched to full-time work for Parousia Media. It was our biggest year yet. January began with a return to the Philippines with Deacon Harold by popular demand! I went there with Deacon and it was great to see the faithful Filipinos again. In March, we welcomed Sarah Swafford, the author of Emotional Virtue.Sarah is a speaker on the Chastity Project and also a presenter on the popular study program, Chosen. It was great to have her in Sydney and Melbourne. We had reached schools, universities, parishes, a pub, a community centre as well as recording new videos and radio.

That same year in May we welcomed both Jason Evert and Trent Horn consecutively. Jason gave twelve talks in three days across three cities, reaching five thousand young people. We partnered with The Chastity Project and again continued the outreach and expansion. We dropped off Jason at Melbourne Airport and welcomed Trent Horn from Catholic Answers an hour later. He started his tour in Melbourne and we just had set up a new Melbourne office as well. Trent Horn gave over ten talks in seven days across two cities. The highlight of this tour was a debate with an atheist from University of Sydney. This was recorded and put up on You Tube and has been a popular debate. It was only May and we had just completed four tours in four cities, including an international tour with Deacon Harold.

In July, we welcomed John Pridmore, the author of *Gangland to Promised Land*. He gave a series of parish missions all over the country. He came with his team: Neil, Catherine and Michael. They were here for three months and we organised over twelve events with him ourselves together with a parish mission reaching over three thousand people and strengthening our partnership. In August, I travelled with Deacon Harold to Jakarta Indonesia and Kuala Lumpur Malaysia over twelve days reaching five thousand people in total across the two countries. We were now in our fifth country and my travels had never been more numerous. At home we were expecting our sixth child, so I had to be home a little more to support my wife. That would be my last international trip for at least a year.

In September at the request of Father Denton we invited German speaker and author Gabriele Kuby to give talks on the global sexual revolution. She spoke in three cities to over two thousand people. Soon after Gabriele returned home we welcomed Christopher West and the Cor Project team. They travelled to three cities: Sydney, Melbourne and Brisbane. Chris gave his two-day intensive course on Theology of the Body to teachers of the Archdiocese of Sydney. He also gave conferences, talks and seminars. We partnered with The Cor Project as a result of this tour. Chris was the keynote speaker at our Fundraising dinner and he gave a great talk on the complementarity of the Male and Female. The fundraiser was another point in our history as we welcomed Karen Manche for Sydney, who replaced the first Karen, and Emily for Melbourne. The Melbourne office was now launched.

Parousia Media was continuing its outreach and expansion with a newly-appointed Victorian manager in John Smyth and a second administrative staff member, Mary Giribaldi. The team had now grown to seven people and the best was yet to come. The first event of the year was Gloria Polo, who was a doctor from Colombia. She miraculously survived a lightning strike and had a near-death experience. She lives to tell the story of how she faced judgement and regretted her abortions. Gloria could not speak English so we had to organise an English translator and thanks to members of the Spanish community we had a very successful visit of five venues in five days, reaching over three thousand people in a single city.

Soon after Gloria Polo visited, Raymond De Souza, who returned for a few days of talks and as usual was hard-hitting and very powerful. In April, we welcomed Father Leo Patalinghug and he was very entertaining. Also known as the cooking priest, Father Leo gave nine presentations in five days in Sydney, Melbourne and Perth. We partnered with Evangelisation Australia in Perth, which was a new group, that was formed by Dr Michael Chong and his close friends. They are doing great work and inviting many of the same speakers we were accustomed to, making it a very healthy collaboration. Once Fr Leo completed his tour we had Dr John Bergsma come to Sydney again in collaboration with Perth. Dr John Bergsma is a biblical professor at the Franciscan University in Steubenville with Scott Hahn. He wrote the series *Bible Basics for Catholics*, which includes the basics of the books on the New Testament and Psalms.

In May, we were contacted from the Asia Pacific team for EWTN talking about how Parousia Media could partner with them for local content. In June, Kevin and I had a meeting in Manila to discuss this proposition and we walked away from that with a camera kit to use for our tours and local content. On the way to Manila I was reading the life of Mother Angelica and I was very moved by that book. She had trusted in Divine Providence the whole time and managed to build a global Catholic network. It was her attitude that inspired me and I felt really comfortable with her model and style. In July, management from EWTN Alabama came to see our offices and decide whether our studio and office would be suitable to use. In the very next month both Kevin and I travelled to Alabama and discussed the partnership. EWTN approved a complete camera kit that would be used to film all of our local footage to submit to the network. We could co-brand these videos for social media and we have been happy to promote the network to anyone who wants to view it. The trip to America also allowed Kevin and me to meet up with the Augustine Institute in Colorado and Focus, who were also there. I got to meet my family again in Miami before returning back to Sydney to get ready for the Fundraiser dinner and Dr Ed Sri.

Dr Ed Sri came for the first time to give twenty one talks over six days and he was a hit. The highlight for Dr Ed Sri would have been his day with all the religious educators, principals and religious coordinators from the schools of the Parramatta Diocese. That has now led to bringing back Dr Sri for the subsequent four years covering each Gospel. We also established a partnership with Ed Sri and have continued to grow his range of resources. He also gave the keynote address at our third fundraiser dinner. This was the first time we made a focused drive on monthly donations. Thank God we raised enough money to hire another staff member and as a result of the dinner and the announcement of the EWTN and Parousia Media partnership we welcomed Miguel Zaragosa to the team as our content manager. He would oversee all the filming, editing and content creation. After the Ed Sri visit, we had a follow up tour with Gabriele Kuby which had led to publishing her book. Finally the Australian Catholic Youth Festival in Sydney was on to close the year. Over eighteen thousand young people turned out to celebrate their Catholic Faith and we had the EWTN team assisting in filming short clips of both the leaders and young people there.

2018 was clearly our biggest year and with so many speakers, the establishment of the EWTN studio, the growth of our You Tube channel and new website. We were tacking things to the next level, thanks be to God. The year started with Christina King who toured with her daughter and gave over fourteen talks in ten days. A highlight of this trip was our first-ever women's retreat and that was so popular. The hundred or more retreatants kept speaking about this event. Christina specialises in healing ministry and she helped so many women on this tour. She reached over three thousand people and travelled to three cities.

The next month Raymond De Souza returned for the fourth time and did some outreach into country towns, so he covered five cities, giving sixteen talks across eight days.

In April we welcomed EWTN, who delivered their camera equipment and set up a brand-new studio for us. We had launched the local content in January but now it went up a level with brand new equipment to use. The You Tube channel had been growing as we had already been releasing five videos a week. Mondays were resources for the week, Tuesdays were endorsements for Parousia Media, Wednesdays were the My Encounter testimonials, Thursdays were Catholic Q and A and finally Friday reflections, with the new series we called Something to think About. Many of these videos were co-branded with EWTN and many Church leaders would begin to notice the work we had been doing.

It was now 2019 and we were preparing for the first ever trip for Jeff Cavins and his wife Emily. There was going to be a big push in establishing as many study groups as possible around the country and faith formation nights each month in parishes as well. We have 140 parishes with resources stands and are beginning to establish a regular routine for annual conferences. If you remember the email I sent to Kevin five years ago about the dream for Australia? Well we are underway in achieving that goal! The next piece to the puzzle is the visit from Dr Scott Hahn with his wife Kimberly and their son David, which we hope to be very soon.

Parousia Brand
MEDIA - LIVE - PARISH

Shifting Gear

Early in 2019, the Parousia team embarked on a process of evaluating what we do, and why we do it. We resolutely peeled away all the layers, exposing everything we do to the bright light of reality. This process has borne tremendous fruit. But the real beauty of this new approach to our work is not the summative outcome, but the way it continually forms and re-forms the Parousia identity and mission. Thinking and acting strategically promises to bear fruit season after season.

A significant shift towards a more strategic way of doing the Parousia business occurred when Ian Smith was appointed to the team in December 2018. Having spent the previous eight years working in senior diocesan roles in Catholic systemic education and as a chancery official, Ian brought a new set of skills and experience to the team. Ian doesn't do anything without a reason, and not just any reason. Inherent goodness is not enough for Ian. Whatever we do has to fit; that is, it must enhance the

stated Parousia identity and mission. The only thing was ...
we hadn't really stated it before.

I have to confess that the sheer pace of doing the business of Parousia is a constant and fierce competitor of thoughtful reflection and analysis of feedback, a competitor that mostly wins. Should I spend more time seeking feedback, learning about leadership and ensuring that each member of the Parousia team reflects on his or her experience and practice? Or, should I press ahead, placing my trust in Him who makes all things possible? How can I do both?

Life at Parousia was frenetic. How could we know whether we were doing what we intended to do? (What did we intend to do?) How could we know whether we were achieving anything meaningful? I couldn't even list off the top of my head the names of everyone Parousia is in partnership with, there are just so many. The number of media and live events Parousia stages annually is in the hundreds. I knew we had to stop, pray and reflect on our purpose. In short, we needed to consolidate before taking another step. A few key ideas emerged from this process.

A spark is lit

First, people attending Parousia events were not getting

what they came for. They were receiving much more. Typically, people came to Parousia events to acquire information. They rightly wanted to be better informed about their faith, the cultural collapse of our society and ways to address it. But what they, and to a large extent, we hadn't anticipated is that they went away transformed. Their relationship with God and connection to the Church had been profoundly deepened. A light had gone on; a spark had been lit. Catholics attending Parousia events came away not just better informed but transformed. Parousia was evangelising Catholics under the pretext of providing training in apologetics.

Second, coming to terms with the evangelising outcome of Parousia events, we needed to know how it worked. We needed to be able to articulate the process. So it goes like this: Parousia, through partners and media, invites people - mostly Catholics already connected to the Church - to an event. It could be a visiting speaker, a retreat, a conference or a video-based study group. Those who attend spend some time in the formation provided by the event, or, in the case of a study group, the multiweek program. As an integral part of the formation, those attending are encouraged to invite others to attend future events and programs. In this way, Catholics are being activated into the mission of the Church. The circle is complete, so to speak, when they actually invite someone to something. This is the Parousia process for making disciples, for activating disciples, to paraphrase Parousia friend Jeff Cavins.

Not Just More Reach, but Greater Impact

Parousia's web-based products, books, DVDs, CDs and other resources served to promote and reinforce the interpersonal experiences Catholics were having at these events. At the core of Parousia's identity and mission was providing opportunities for Catholics to be transformed into disciples who were now active participants in the mission of the Church. I understood that Parousia not only had reach, but impact.

Ian Smith, who was appointed as our National Director of Evangelisation, worked with me in 2019 to understand the history of Parousia Media and identify its mission and vision. I went through all the history I have shared in this chapter. Seeing the need of the Church and the work we have done over the years we came up with identifying the limitations with the name Parousia Media. The word media limits us to that one area when, clearly, we are doing more than just media, given the events we host and our close work with parishes also. We have officially dropped the word 'media' and are now simply called 'Parousia', which provides three service streams of Media, Live and Parish. To explain all this further, we developed a prospectus and updated the website to reflect this new brand. The logo got a refresh and we now have a clearer vision of what we focus on and where we are going.

The work over the years has now reached over 250,000 people at our events alone, not including the 400,000 views on YouTube or 25,000 likes on Facebook, as well as the hits on EWTN and other partners who promote our work. In total, over 1,000,000 people have been reached either in person or online via the work of Parousia and its partners. The numbers look good on the surface, but this is only a drop in the ocean. Now that we better understand the process of evangelisation, we are determined to reach vastly more people than we currently serve. Here is the letter I wrote, taken from our prospectus and website. It also explains further our understanding of the urgent context of the mission and how we see Parousia helping to meet the needs of Catholics.

A Nation in Retreat

There is ample evidence that Australians and the Western world are turning their backs on God. We are made in his image, but can't decide what male and female are, let alone what they mean for marriage, family and human flourishing.

Remembrance of God in Australia and other Western countries has become a nostalgic concern rather than a neuralgic one. Meanwhile, the decline in religious belief and practice is, according to the statistical trend, terminal.

Religious Practice in Decline

Nationally, 39,020 fewer Catholics attended Sunday Mass in Australia in 2016 compared to 2011. Diocesan Mass attendance rates are between a high of 15.7% in the Archdiocese of Sydney and 6.7% in the Archdiocese of Hobart, with a national average of 11.8% in 2016, down from 12.2% in 2011. Impressively, the Maronite Eparchy, records a Sunday Mass attendance rate of 49.6%. Just as telling as attendance rates is the obvious lack of formation and missionary intent among Mass-going Catholics. These brothers and sisters need accessible, high-quality formative resources in order to build a daily routine around prayer and service.

Turning the Tide

The good statistical news is that the 623,656 Catholics who attend Mass each Sunday in Australia are poised to be drafted into a new spiritual force. Researchers provide a long list of reasons self-identifying Catholics do not attend Mass, from children's sport to the abuse scandal. No doubt these factors are culturally powerful, but I submit that the main reason is not having experienced the transforming love of Jesus. And yet, I see these transformations every day at Parousia study groups, apologetics classes, women's retreats and international speakers' events.

What are the Three Major Things We Do?

Evangelising

"Go therefore and make disciples of all nations ..."
(Matt 28:19).

Most people are not aware that a personal relationship with God is even possible. Evangelisation isn't the only thing the Church does, but if we fail at evangelisation, we will ultimately fail at everything.

Parousia Intends to Evangelise by:
- Recognising that evangelisation is a process, not a

145

program or an event;
- Supporting local and interpersonal initiatives; and
- Cultivating a culture of invitation.

Forming

"Always be prepared to make a defense to anyone who calls you to account for the hope that is in you."
1 (Pet. 3:15).

Parousia believes in the power of dynamic preaching to transform non-believers into honest enquirers, and committed Catholics into saints-in-the-making. Parousia will continue to be a trusted source of current Catholic literature and multimedia, now extending its range into streaming and podcasting of new content through the acquisition of Cradio. Study groups that make effective use of video resources will be a feature of the national Parousia brand. Video resourcing provides content and structure that facilitates the building of community and deepening of friendships with God; so that Catholics are not just better informed, but are transformed, in Christ.

Parousia Intends to Form by:
- Inviting, inspiring and equipping Catholics for the mission of evangelisation;
- Creating, sourcing and distributing trustworthy

Catholic resources; and

- Making accessible in person and via multimedia dynamic local and international speakers.

Leading

"For the Son of man also came not to be served, but to serve, and to give his life as a ransom for many."
(Mk 10:45).

If you want to bring people to the knowledge and love of Jesus, His Church and His mission, then we want to help in whatever way we can, if we can. We want to bring people into lifelong friendship with Christ and if we can do it with you, then all the better.

Parousia Intends to Model Catholic Apostolate by:
- Collaborating with parishes, schools, dioceses and ministries that share our zeal for evangelisation and formation;
- Inviting Catholics who are connected with the Church to actively join the mission; and
- Engaging in a continuous conversation with partners and supporters.

So, What's Next for Parousia?

1. New and Improved

In 2019 and beyond, Parousia Media intends to build on its brand of trustworthy Catholic speakers and resources by serving the Church through evangelisation, formation and leadership.

Parousia Media is expanding horizons beyond media; extending, rather than forfeiting, its foundations. Parousia Media will henceforth be, simply, Parousia.

2. Parousia Parish

Launching in the second half of 2019, Parousia Parish is a service to support parish priests and parents. Parousia believes that evangelising and formation begins, and is most effective, in the family home and the parish. Within these structures, it is the leadership of the priest in the parish and husbands and wives in the family that will make or break the future of the Church in Australia and beyond.

3. Parousia Training

Enhancing the quality of our reach by providing a) designed-for-purpose professional learning for teachers, school and system leaders, and b) leadership training for study program graduates who would like to run programs in their homes and parishes.

Conclusion

The Next Chapter - Now This is Getting Serious
Will you join me on this Adventurous Journey?

You have just gone on a journey with me about my family history and some specific stories with a lesson for all of us on both spectrums. We are all called to a specific vocation and unique calling. I encourage you to find your calling in life. Once you do find it you will truly experience freedom. I invite you to join me on the mission of fulfilling Christ's last command of making disciples of all nations.

It is my prayer that the work of Parousia fulfills this mission and that it reaches as many souls as possible. Parousia is here to not just inform but to transform. Our purpose is to evangelise, form and lead in a Church that is so desperately trying to reach a hurting world. We want to take full advantage of the Media in all forms as well as live events and of course support the parishes, as it is the parish that is the second home of all Catholics.

Finally I invite you to be in touch with me via www. parousiamedia.com and to keep up to date with all that is going on in the Parousia world. Please pray for me, as I, and the team at Parousia, will continue to pray for you. God bless you.

Biography

Charbel Raish is married to Christine and they have been blessed with seven children. Charbel has a passion for helping people get closer to discovering the fullness of truth and invites anyone who is willing to help him on this mission of evangelisation through Parousia.

Charbel has two Degrees – Master of Arts and Theological Studies from the University of Notre Dame in Sydney, and his undergraduate Degree in Personal Development and Physical Education from the Australian College of Physical Education in Homebush Bay. He has over ten years of experience as both a Physical Education teacher and Religion teacher for primary and secondary schools.

Currently Charbel works full-time with Parousia, his greatest passion, which specialises in Faith Formation resources and events. Over 350,000 people have been evangelised through the work of Parousia Media and well over one million people have been reached overall including online.

Charbel gives talks on Evangelisation and Faith Formation, the Bible timeline, as well as a personal testimony on how Islam led him to Christ. He coordinates study courses such as 'A Quick Journey through the Bible' and 'Chosen' – an introductory study of the Catholic Faith.

Based in Sydney, may travel internationally upon request.

Be part of
PAROUSIA

We would like to invite you to be a member of the Parousia team. Parousia cannot activate Catholics and turn the tide without your support.

Our ultimate goal is to evangelise to all nations, and claim for the children of the world.

For more information, please contact:

Parousia
Ph: +61 2 9651 0375
office@parousiamedia.com
www.parousiamedia.com

The Parousia
Partners & Brands

Access the best Catholic content from around the
world. We partner with reliable Catholic sources
like EWTN, Augustine Institute, Ascension Press,
Chastity Project, St. Joseph Communications,
Catholic Answers, and more!

other partners

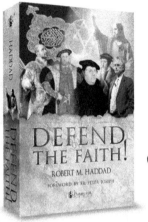

20 Answers: Islam

- What are the basic teachings of Islam?
- How does the Quran compare with the Bible?
- Does Islam really encourage violence in God's name, or is it a religion of peace?
- Can dialogue between Christians and Muslims foster a believers' alliance against secularism and the Culture of Death?

In this booklet you'll find smart, solid answers to these questions and many more. 20 Answers: Islam looks inside the religion of Mohammad to reveal what its own theological authorities teach, cutting through the ignorance and wishful thinking that are too common in our culture to spell out Islam's challenges to the Christian West–past, present, and future.

For Australia and New Zealand, please contact:

Parousia
PO Box 59 Galston, NSW 2159
Ph: +61 2 9651 0375

office@parousiamedia.com
www.parousiamedia.com

INSIDE ISLAM

Inside Islam: A Guide for Catholics utilizes a popular question-and-answer format so that all Catholics—both the theological novice and the well-catechized—can learn the basics of Islam. Co-authors Robert Spencer and Daniel Ali, a convert from Islam, give you a solid understanding of Islam's unique teachings including:

- The Islamic view of God
- The role of Jesus in Islamic theology
- Islam's controversial theology of jihad, or "holy war"
- Why Islam's strong beliefs are so attractive to secularized Western societies
- The role of women in Islam

Inside Islam is an essential resource for anyone who wants to know more about this historic religion from the Middle East. After reading this book, you will have a better understanding of the issues discussed every day in the news.

For Australia and New Zealand, please contact:

Parousia
PO Box 59 Galston, NSW 2159   office@parousiamedia.com
Ph: +61 2 9651 0375   www.parousiamedia.com

Related Topic Available

ABBA OR ALLAH

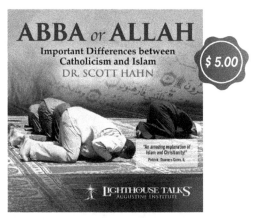

Audio CD

In this informative talk, Dr. Scott Hahn explores some of the most important beliefs that distinguish Christianity from Islam. He explains that while both religions trace themselves back to Abraham, the differences, including our understanding of God as Father, are not insignificant. With charity, balance, and candor, Dr. Hahn shows us how Islam presents the most formidable challenge to Christianity in the Third millennium.

For Australia and New Zealand, please contact:

Parousia
PO Box 59 Galston, NSW 2159   office@parousiamedia.com
Ph: +61 2 9651 0375   www.parousiamedia.com

Proclaiming the fullness of Truth

Parousia
PO Box 59 Galston, NSW 2159
Ph: +61 2 9651 0375
office@parousiamedia.com
www.parousiamedia.com

9 780648 198437